MW01056847

DATE DUE

APR 1 3 2010	
DEC 0 1 2011	
NOV 1 6 2010	
SEP 2 3 2011	
SEP 2 9 2011	

GAYLORD   PRINTED IN U.S.A.

EMPIRE STYLEBOOK OF INTERIOR DESIGN

EMPIRE STYLEBOOK OF INTERIOR DESIGN

All 72 Plates from the
"Recueil de décorations intérieures"
with New English Text

Charles Percier and Pierre Fontaine

DOVER PUBLICATIONS, INC.
NEW YORK

Published in Canada by General Publishing Company, Ltd., 30 Lesmill Road,
Don Mills, Toronto, Ontario.
Published in the United Kingdom by Constable and Company, Ltd., 3 The
Lanchesters, 162–164 Fulham Palace Road, London W6 9ER.

This Dover edition, first published in 1991, is a new complete translation of
the original edition of *Recueil de décorations intérieures*, published by the authors
(Percier and Fontaine) in Paris, 1812. For the full original title, see pages vi and
vii; for further bibliographic data, see the new, specially written Introduction to
the Dover Edition. The plates have been reproduced directly from the originals.
The translation and Introduction are by Stanley Appelbaum.

Manufactured in the United States of America
Dover Publications, Inc., 31 East 2nd Street, Mineola, N.Y. 11501

Library of Congress Cataloging-in-Publication Data

Percier, Charles, 1764–1838.
    [Recueil de décorations intérieures. English]
    Empire stylebook of interior design : all 72 plates from the Recueil de
décorations intérieures, with new English text / Charles Percier and Pierre
Fontaine.
        p.   cm.
    ISBN 0-486-26754-7
    1. Decoration and ornament—France—Empire style.   2. Interior deco-
ration—France—History—19th century.   I. Fontaine, Pierre François
Léonard, 1762–1853.   II. Title.
NK1449.A1P4713   1991
747.24'09'034—dc20   91-7520
                                                                              CIP

Introduction to the Dover Edition

1. The Authors

PIERRE-FRANÇOIS-LÉONARD FONTAINE (1762–1853), from Pontoise (not far from Paris, to the northwest), came from a family of architects and builders. The Parisian Charles Percier (1764–1838) was the son of a swing-bridge keeper. By the late 1770s they were studying art and architecture in Paris and probably met in 1779. A sojourn of several years in Rome from 1786 on (Fontaine on his own modest resources, Percier as winner of a Prix de Rome) was crucial both professionally and personally. The two young men studied not only ancient ruins but also Renaissance buildings, expanding their horizons immeasurably. They also made a pact of lifelong friendship that should never be intruded on by marriage; even though the two died fifteen years apart, they (and a third friend of the Roman days, Bernier) were buried in the same tomb.

Back in the seething revolutionary Paris of the early 1790s, they looked for work. One of their early patrons was the celebrated furniture maker Georges Jacob, for whom they did designs. A decoration assignment at the Opéra opened the door to numerous commissions, for the rest of that decade, to decorate the lavish residences of the speculators, financiers, diplomats and ministers spawned by the Revolution. One of these, for whom they worked in 1799, recommended them to his Parisian neighbor, Joséphine Bonaparte, wife of the rising general who was already challenging the government of the Directors and would oust them, by the end of that year, to become First Consul and the master of France.

For the First Consul, in 1800–1802, Percier and Fontaine redecorated the château of Malmaison outside Paris; the library, music room and bedroom they designed are still extant and are the best surviving witness to their perfection of the special offshoot of Neoclassicism that was to become known as the Empire style (Napoleon made himself Emperor in 1804). For the remainder of the Napoleonic era—although they did not always see eye to eye with the temperamental and often unreasonable potentate—the two partners were to be official government architects and decorators, designing or redesigning residences of the Emperor himself (including the château at St.-Cloud [since demolished] in 1801–1802, and the Tuileries palace [since demolished] from 1801 onward) and residences of the imperial clan in France and many other parts of Europe (their magnificent Gabinete de Platino in the Casa del Labrador on the grounds of the Aranjuez palace outside Madrid is still extant), and working on such other Napoleonic projects as the colonnade, courtyard facades and museum rooms of the Louvre palace (from 1805 on, parts still extant), the adjoining Arc de Triomphe du Carrousel (1806–1808, extant) and the arcaded Rue de Rivoli joining the Louvre to the Tuileries (from 1804 on), not to mention the décor for Napoleon's coronation in 1804 and his marriage to Marie-Louise of Austria in 1810.

Fontaine was the more active partner, making the business arrangements, doing most of the large-scale planning and making appearances on the construction sites. Percier, who was sickly, stayed in the office and was responsible for the exquisite detailing and finish. He devoted himself chiefly to teaching from 1812 on, and retired in 1814. Fontaine, who—like Georges Jacob and other artists, not to mention the perennial statesman Talleyrand—was never seriously penalized for his adherence to earlier regimes—continued to work for Louis XVIII (the Chapelle Expiatoire), Charles X (the Palais-Royal) and Louis-Philippe (the Théâtre Français, etc.) until his retirement in 1848.

2. The Book and Its Significance

The influence of Percier and Fontaine and their special "Empire" brand of Neoclassicism in architecture, interior design and furnishings (a combination of severity and pomp; a more strictly archeological approach to form and detail than had been the case hitherto, with a greater emphasis on earlier Greek models—often mislabeled "Etruscan" at the time—than on Imperial Roman monuments; an admixture of French and Italian Renaissance elements, with an additional *soupçon* of Gothic; a strong reliance on Egyptian motifs, popularized by Napoleon's Egyptian campaign of 1798–1799; the combination of mahogany and ormolu; etc.) was spread by their personal teaching (their pupils were also active in countries other than France), but even more so by the stream of publications they issued from 1798 on.

Of these books, none was more influential than the *Recueil de décorations intérieures* ("Collection of Interior Decorations," the first book ever to use that phrase in its title), a set of 72 plates illustrating the authors' work in all genres. The plates appeared in 12 installments of six sheets each, the first of which was issued in 1801; the book was completed in 1812, when all 72 plates were bound together, along with a "Prefatory Essay" (Discours préliminaire) and a description of the plates. (For the full title of the publication, see pages vi and vii. A second edition appeared in 1827.)

The plates are in outline engraving, a style that had been made popular by the English artist and pottery designer John Flaxman in his illustrations of Homer and Dante (1794) and was used frequently in the period to illustrate art books (Flaxman, as well as the English interior designer Thomas Hope and the Italian sculptor Antonio Canova—books by Hope and Canova were illustrated in the same technique—were all close personal friends of Percier). For some of the plates in the *Recueil*, watercolor drawings by Fontaine—obviously the models for the engravings—have survived.

The plates depict many of the authors' outstanding achievements: furniture and interior decoration for plutocrats in France (plates 1–7, 9,

12–20, 22, 23, 25–27, 30, 32–40, 44, 50, 54, 57, 59, 60 and 65) and abroad (plates 8, 10, 11, 21, 24, 28, 29, 31 and 58)—note that the early plates 1–18 (but not the corresponding plate descriptions, prepared much later) use the revolutionary title *citoyen*, "citizen," instead of "Monsieur" (the title *maître*, used in a few plates, indicates a lawyer); the redecoration of Malmaison and other work for Joséphine (plates 41, 42, 46, 52 and 55); the redecoration at St.-Cloud (plates 39 [no. 3] and 47); the work at the Tuileries (plates 43, 45, 48, 49, 51, 53, 56 and 66); the "platinum" cabinet for Aranjuez (plates 61–64); and the museum installations in the Louvre (plates 67–72). (Some rooms in the Louvre had been used as museum galleries even before the Revolution in the eighteenth century; Napoleon, with his customary self-aggrandizement, created a Musée Napoléon there and installed the masterpieces he had plundered on his European campaigns. After Waterloo, the French were forced to disgorge, and the Venus of the Venus Room, plates 67 to 71—none other than the Medici Venus—is now back at the Uffizi in Florence.)

A number of other artists are mentioned in the plate captions and descriptions. The Lacour who engraved the headpiece to the Prefatory Essay is probably Pierre Lacour *fils* (1778–1859), who worked in Paris from 1798 to 1814 before returning to his native Bordeaux. The brothers Jacob mentioned in connection with plates 15, 16 and 23 were Georges (II) Jacob (1768–1802) and François-Honoré-Georges Jacob (1770–1841, retired 1825); they and their father, Georges Jacob (1739–1814), the early employer of Percier and Fontaine, were the premier *ébénistes* of the period. When Georges II died, his father, who had retired in 1796, became the partner of his surviving son, who changed his own name (and the firm name) to Jacob-Desmalter. The only other furniture maker mentioned in the *Recueil* is Alexandre Regnier (Régnier?, caption to plate 14). Contemporary painters mentioned are Pierre Prud'hon (1758–1823, description of plate 47), Anne-Louis Girodet de Roucy Trioson (1767–1824, description of plates 61–64) and (in the same description) Jean-Joseph-Xavier Bidauld (or Bidault, 1758–1846) and Jean-Thomas Thibault (or Thibaut, 1757–1826). The great French Renaissance sculptor Jean Goujon (c. 1510–c. 1568) is mentioned in the descriptions of plates 49 and 72, and his contemporary, the architect Pierre Lescot (c. 1515–1578), in the latter description.

The admirable Prefatory Essay clearly defines the extremely advanced views of Percier and Fontaine on total unified control of interior decoration down to the last detail of design and placement (the essay has been seen as the progenitor of the twentieth century's designer cult) and their wish to combine functionalism (though not nearly as spare as that of the Bauhaus and the International Style!) with beauty, while not neglecting the gains made by modern industry.

The plate descriptions ("Explanatory Table . . .") indicate the original color and materials of many of the works of art, give some notion of the physical and esthetic constraints and special instructions that were inherent in some of the authors' commissions, and supply further insights into the craftsmanship and up-to-the-moment technology involved. (For instance, the large sheets of glass, mirrored or clear, called for in several projects were a specialty of the Parisian manufacturers of the time. For the use of air-current lamps, see plate 39; for an example of prefabrication, see plates 61–64.)

Some features and principles of the Percier and Fontaine style are not spelled out in so many words, but can be detected in the book: for example, the creative concealment of such utilitarian items as stoves within pillars and other constructions that appear to be merely decorative, and the insistence on the "isolation" of pieces of furniture—intended to be free-standing, central and viewed from all sides rather than ranged alongside a wall.

In the present edition, some of the plates have had to be reduced. The only reduced plate bearing a scale of size, however, is plate 68, which appears at 78% of original size. Naturally, the indications *mètre* and *décimètre* on a few plates are to be understood as meter (39.37 inches) and decimeter (one-tenth of the foregoing), while *pied* is virtually the same as our foot.

All the text in the present volume following this introduction, except for a few editorial brackets, is a full new translation of the words of Percier and Fontaine themselves.

Readers who wish a further analysis, brief but incisive, of the characteristics of Empire architecture should consult Robin Middleton and David Watkin, *Neoclassical and 19th Century Architecture/2: The Diffusion and Development of Classicism and the Gothic Revival*, Electa/Rizzoli, N.Y., 1980. For the interior-design aspects, see Charles McCorquodale, *The History of Interior Decoration*, Phaidon, Oxford, 1983, and Peter Thornton, *Authentic Decor: The Domestic Interior, 1620–1920*, Viking, N.Y., 1984. For the furniture aspect, see the article by Serge Grandjean in Helena Hayward (ed.), *World Furniture: An Illustrated History from Earliest Times*, Crescent Books, N.Y., 1990 (earlier: Hamlyn, London, 1965). In every one of these accounts, the names of Percier and Fontaine are of paramount significance.

EMPIRE STYLEBOOK
OF INTERIOR DESIGN

[Translation of the engraved title plate (opposite). (The full typographic title of the 1812 edition was exactly the same down through the word "dessins"/"drawings.")]

COLLECTION
OF INTERIOR DECORATIONS
INCLUDING ALL MATTERS HAVING REGARD
TO FURNISHINGS,
SUCH AS

VASES, TRIPODS, CANDELABRA, INCENSE BURNERS, CHANDELIERS, GIRANDOLES, LAMPS,
CANDLESTICKS, FIREPLACES, FIREPLACE GARNITURES, STOVES, CLOCKS, TABLES, SECRETARIES, BEDS,
SOFAS, ARMCHAIRS, CHAIRS, STOOLS, MIRRORS, SCREENS, ETC., ETC., ETC.

DESIGNED BY C. PERCIER AND P. F. L. FONTAINE,
EXECUTED AFTER THEIR DRAWINGS.

Deposited at the National Library.

This work will contain
72 plates divided into
12 fascicles, each of
6 sheets.

The price is 4 francs per fascicle
engraved in line on *papier de France*,
9 francs on *papier de Hollande*, 30
francs with washes and tints.

Paris, Year IX, 1801.
For sale by the authors, rue Montmarte 219;
Ducamp, stationer, rue St.-Honoré, corner of rue de Valois 167;
Joubert, printseller, rue de Sorbonne; Pougens, bookseller, quai de Voltaire;
Coeffier, rue de Coq. St.-Honoré; and all dry-goods merchants.

RECUEIL

DE DÉCORATIONS INTÉRIEURES
COMPRENANT TOUT CE QUI A RAPPORT
A L'AMEUBLEMENT
COMME

VASES, TRÉPIEDS, CANDELABRES, CASSOLETTES, LUSTRES, GIRANDOLES, LAMPES,
CHANDELIERS, CHEMINÉES, FEUX, POÊLES, PENDULES, TABLES, SECRÉTAIRES,
LITS, CANAPÉS, FAUTEUILS, CHAISES, TABOURETS, MIROIRS, ECRANS, &c. &c. &c.

COMPOSÉS PAR C. PERCIER ET P. F. L. FONTAINE.
EXÉCUTÉS SUR LEURS DESSINS.

Déposé à la Bibliothéque Nationale.

Cet Ouvrage contiendra
72 Planches divisées en
12 Cahiers de chacun
6 feuilles.

Le prix est de 4.f le Cahier
Gravé au Trait, sur Papier
de France, 9.f sur Papier de
Hollande, 30.f Lavé et Colorié.

PARIS AN IX. M DCCCI.
Se vend chez les Auteurs rue Montmartre N.º 219
Ducamp M.d Papetier rue S.t Honoré au coin de celle de Vallois N.º 157
chez   Joubert M.d d'Estampes rue de Sorbonne. Pougens Libraire Quai de Voltaire,
Coeffier rue du Coq S.t Honoré et chez touts les M.ds de nouveautés.

Par Percier et Fontaine.

Gravé par Lacour.

Prefatory Essay [Discours préliminaire]

IN PRESENTING TO THE PUBLIC THE collection of furniture and interior decorations that comprise this work, the originals having been executed to our designs at various times, we are by no means claiming to offer artists any models for imitation. Our ambition would be satisfied if, in this field that is so mutable and so subject to the vicissitudes of opinion and caprice, we could take some credit for contributing to the dissemination and the upholding of the principles of taste that we have derived from ancient [Greco-Roman] art, and that we believe are linked, albeit by a less apparent chain, to those general laws of truth, simplicity and beauty that should eternally govern every production in the realm of imitation [artistic creation, viewed as a copy of nature, life and reality].

Within this empire, the theory of taste cannot draw a line between the most minor and the most grandiose artistic productions. They are joined by a common bond. They influence each other actively and reciprocally. Whatever may be the predominant style of imitation and creation at a given time or in a given country, the enlightened eye of the connoisseur discerns it, follows its effect and consequences in the greatest undertakings of the arts of painting, sculpture and architecture, as in the minor products of the industrial arts, which are associated with all the needs and pleasures of society.

Who cannot discern the direction taken by intelligence and taste in each period by studying the details of its domestic utensils, its objects of luxury or necessity, to which the craftsman has involuntarily given the stamp of the forms, outlines and types customary in his day? Do we not count the generations, so to say, by the forms of tables, chairs, furniture, tapestries? Is not Raphael's genius observable in all the decorative objects that he influenced? What collector does not pay a high price for all those scattered remains of the taste of the sixteenth century, that century which, after a long barren period, proved to be a sort of offshoot of classical antiquity, and which subsequent centuries, despite all efforts of the innovative mind, have failed to equal, all the while believing they were surpassing it? Three or four periods of taste, manner and style have followed since, and always the forms of furniture have accorded perfectly with the genius that directed the inventions of the architect, the sculptor and the painter. The metalwork of the age of Louis XIV is imbued with the taste of Le Brun. Boulle's armoires and pedestal tables have the contours, profiles and escutcheons of Mansard. The eighteenth century displays its petty, false and insignificant taste in the gilding of its woodwork, the outlines of its mirrors, the jig-sawing of its overdoors and carriages, etc., as in the mixtilinear plans of its buildings and the manneredness of its painted compositions.

Nevertheless, the end of that century, through a conjunction of causes that it would be needless to describe here, saw its taste not only change but pass quite abruptly from one extreme to the other.

Architecture—which in general sets the tone for the other arts and especially for the decorative arts—weary, as it were, of all the innovations by which for two centuries its realm was thought to have been extended, found itself restored to the simplicity of ancient taste, and in fact the most ancient taste of the Greeks.

The great number of temples with columns of the Doric order without base that were brought to light again by the discoveries of travelers produced a sort of sudden revolution in that art. Before those monuments were well known, they were considered as belonging to the childhood of art. After they had been more closely examined, they were held to be an architecture suitable only for use in buildings of a heavy, vulgar type. But after it became clear that such architecture existed throughout Greece, and in temples of the most glorious period, opinion changed. The taste for things Greek had become stylish; Doric without base was applied to everything. Soon the numerous discoveries in every area of antiquity led to the abandonment of the forms and taste that had long been dominant.

It was realized that the above-mentioned connection between works of fine art and industrial products had also been achieved by the people of antiquity: the smallest fragments of their utensils, furniture, paintings and ornaments were collected. The excavations undertaken in the cities of Herculaneum and Pompeii, by bringing back a multitude of objects that had once formed part of the furnishings and interior decoration of houses, increased more and more that taste for the imitation of antiquity. All this, taken together with the change that had come over architecture, contributed to the reformation of modern furniture design. Simple lines, clean contours and correct forms replaced the mixtilinear, the contorted and the irregular.

The discoveries just discussed spread the taste for ancient art all the more rapidly thanks to engravings, which were used to disseminate drawings of those monuments, large or small. These sets of engravings made their way into every industrial-art studio and, with the slightest invention of ancient taste becoming the property of anyone seeking to rejuvenate the products of his labor, antiquity came to be the most fruitful source for the spirit of fashion.

If we are sometimes astonished at the great number of objects of art and taste that time and destruction have been unable to eliminate from the legacy of antiquity, we are soon led to be even more astonished at the immensity of the losses we have sustained. Without the cities of Herculaneum and Pompeii, what would we know about the details of ancient domestic arts, of their furniture, of the taste in ornament of their interiors, of the layout of their houses, of their habits in luxury spending? These cities, of Greek origin, were still following Greek practice at the time of their destruction. We find in them stylistic nuances and decorative finesse that are more in line with Greek taste than with Roman pomp. And yet certain eccentric features already seem to point to an era in which simplicity had gone out of fashion, in which the artist was responding not so much to the inspiration of nature as to the need to cajole with novelties a spirit that was beginning to be surfeited with the truly beautiful.

Is it not really regrettable that similar discoveries could not be made in Greece itself, and in such a way that we could grasp what the taste in furnishings must have been like in one of its major cities and at one of the best periods of its arts?

The art of engraving, which, like that of printing, has the power to disseminate works, will perhaps also have the advantage of making them imperishable. But another benefit conferred by that art is its power to preserve in albums of prints a multitude of things that are ephemeral by nature and are doomed to leave behind only memories, the permanence of which no [verbal] tradition can guarantee.

Only great works of art can cross great intervals of time. But how is one to perpetuate the memory of what is called the taste of a country and an era, embodied in that innumerable multitude of objects replacing one another constantly, executed in light or fragile materials, and reflecting so clearly the character, manners and opinions of their makers? What we understand by the term furnishings forms part of this class of more or less ephemeral productions.

If, since the invention of engraving, that art had been used to gather and transmit all the creations of the type we have been discussing, would it not be a great pleasure to survey the course of the intelligence and taste embodied in these works for a period of three centuries? How interesting it would be to follow the ups and downs of inventiveness ceaselessly turning in a kind of circle, so often mistaken even with regard to the impulse it receives and imparts in turn, imagining that it is ascending because it is moving onward, and unconsciously returning to its point of departure!

Engravings give only an imperfect idea of the masterpieces of imitation; and, even though in this respect the means of preservation they offer are not to be disdained, nevertheless it will be agreed that the objects of taste, luxury and ornament that are our subject can receive much greater services from that art.

It is therefore partially with this in view that we have felt it helpful to use engravings to assemble those works of ours in the area of furnishings that, either from the importance of their intended purpose or from the rank of those who commissioned them, may be regarded as suitable testimonies of the manner of seeing, composing and decorating at the present time.

If this example can encourage other artists to entrust to engraving, in this way, the works done under their direction, we will be able to credit ourselves with having launched a type of annals of the taste of our generation in this field.

But, as we have already indicated, we have had another viewpoint in mind in publishing this collection. In works of ornament and decoration it is possible to make a distinction between species and genus, and to consider them separately. The genus is by no means our own; it belongs completely to the people of antiquity; and, just as our sole merit would lie in the conformity of our productions to the ancient spirit, so our real purpose in presenting them to the public is to do all that is in our power to prevent the mania for novelty from corrupting or destroying the principles on the basis of which others will no doubt surpass us.

Despite the kind of predominance that the taste for antiquity seems to have gained for some years now, we cannot disregard the fact that it only owes a large part of this ascendancy to the power exerted by fashion in modern nations.

The power of fashion, that great guiding spirit of works of art, owes its influence to three causes: one being a moral cause, connected with the love of change implanted in the human mind; the second, a social cause, dependent upon our social customs, in which the relations between the sexes, mutual visits and gatherings exert a very active influence on the desire to please; the third, a commercial cause, linked to the interest all artisans have in making luxury items become obsolete in order to replace products more often and increase their sales.

Of these three causes, it seems to us that the first, which is general, is the only one whose action is traceable in antiquity. But it must be said that this action did not produce the same effects at the time. The love of change is so inherent in the human mind that the arts, far from deeming themselves capable of resisting it, are precisely the most devoted servants of that natural inclination. But there are two ways of accommodating that penchant: one way is to conserve in every object that which is its original type, principle or necessary reason and, without falsifying its fundamental nature, to vary the accessory forms, the details, the circumstances, so that the essential is invariable and it is only the accident that changes. This was the way of antiquity in all its works from the largest to the smallest, from the temple to the clay pot. The other way is totally capricious, affecting the fundamental nature of an object even more than its form, the principal features more than the accessories. That is the character of the taste of the moderns, who, possessed in all areas by an incredible mania for change, have sought in all fields of art merely to do something different from the past, without concern for the basic reasons, natural principles and laws that convention prescribes for each object.

This mania for change is no longer linked to the universal cause traceable to the nature of our mind, that need for variety which is itself the fruitful basis of mental activity. Its origin is to be sought in the two other principles we have mentioned.

The mode of existence and the customs of modern societies, which put every individual on show in places of promenade, conversation, gaming and pleasure, have aroused to the highest degree the wish to please, on the one hand, and the desire to distinguish oneself, on the other. Hence that supremacy of fashion in all that pertains to dress, personal adornment and manners; hence that constantly recurring pressure which leads the majority to imitate the tone-setting minority, and the minority to drop a practice as soon as it becomes widespread. Ridicule is the weapon of fashion, and the greater the number of spectators, the more powerful the weapon. And since, for sensible people, it is not worthwhile either to avoid ridicule or to court it, the current of fashion meets no resistance. Everyone yields to it more or less readily, and conforms to it in a multitude of things that, directly or remotely, vitiate the imitation of the true and the beautiful.

The more the taste and pleasures of what is now called "society" have increased, the more has the pressure of fashion extended its power, and there is almost nothing in domestic interiors that is not subordinated to it. Decoration and furnishing are becoming for houses what clothing is for people: in this area, too, everything becomes obsolete and in just a few years is considered outmoded and ridiculous. The industrial arts, which work together with architecture in the embellishment of buildings, receive the same impulse from the spirit of fashion, and no sort of beauty or talent can assure all these objects of taste a duration longer than the time necessary to find a new taste that will replace them.

We will allow the reader to imagine the consequences for the other arts of imitation under the influence of such domination. But no one will deny that architecture must be affected first and most directly.

The models for that art do not find in nature the actuality, reality and materiality inherent in the models for sculpture or painting. Although the tangible models for those two latter arts can always be infected by the spirit of fashion—not the models themselves, but the manner of seeing and imitating them—it will nevertheless be true that defects of imitation here will be more easily exposed through a comparison with nature.

But that in nature which is the model for architecture exists in an abstract and analogic region accessible only to intelligence, reason and feeling. Architecture imitates nature only insofar as it works in the same way: her reasons, her conventions, her understanding of the goal in mind—these are the true models for the art.

To do everything rationally, to do everything in such a way that the rationality is evident and justifies the means employed—this is the first principle of architecture.

On the other hand, the first principle of fashion is to do everything for no other reason than to do something different. Not only is this taste not directed, in creating a product, by any regard for the purpose of the product; most of the time it delights in contradicting the purpose. The forms or needs of the body are not the rationale for the forms of clothing, for people do not get dressed to clothe themselves but to adorn themselves. Furniture is not made under any necessity that prescribes its form. Fashion changes from the straight to the crooked, from the simple to the compound, and vice versa. This is all too true of the history of modern architecture and its ups and downs.

Even though we have stated that that art has returned to more proper principles for some years now, we are by no means convinced that this improvement can be maintained.

To prove that this return to a better taste is largely due to the power of fashion, one need only observe, in all our surroundings, the disorderly abuse being made of the most beautiful forms, of the most beautiful creative ideas, in objects to which they are least suited.

For example, if sphinxes and Egyptian-style terms [terminal statues], because of the severity of their forms and their allegorical meaning, can be suitable for given purposes in certain objects of architecture or furnishings, before long we shall see every shop sign, every overdoor, in the Egyptian style. If the lightness and playful associations of the arabesque are suited to small compartments and fit in with pieces whose size and character require only lightheartedness, soon, if fashion takes over that taste, the arabesque will become the universal ornament. Thus we have seen the Doric order without base, which is used for temples, become the order in shops, guardrooms and the most commonplace structures imaginable.

The factor that popularizes the concepts and forms of products in this way is neither a truer feeling nor a more popularly enlightened taste: they are wanted for no other reason than the one that makes people want the cut of garments or the hair style of the moment. These things are not wanted because they are thought beautiful, but they are thought beautiful because they are wanted. Therefore, they most promptly undergo the fate of all products of fashion. Industry gets hold of them, reproduces them in a thousand inexpensive ways, puts them within reach of the slenderest purse. All sorts of falsifications denature and devalue them. Plaster stands in for marble, paper plays the role of painting, cardboard imitates the work of scissors, glass is substituted for gems, sheet metal replaces massive metal, varnishes masquerade as porphyry. This results in a first abuse, which proceeds from the very spirit of fashion: to cheapen that which becomes common, to lower quickly in the public's estimation things that are found to be debased by the most trivial uses; for nothing can prevent the most beautiful works from losing part of their beauty in this way. The same thing would happen even to the works of nature; and if beauty were more common among them, one must believe that our soul would be less affected, less touched by its charm.

But the most serious abuse connected with the unceasing prostitution of the creations of art and taste, is to rob them—by shoddy work, by fraudulence of materials and by routine or mechanical production methods—of that perfection of execution, that precious finish, that touch of original feeling which theory, and theory alone, distinguishes from the acts of conception and creation but which is really inseparable from them. The habit of seeing a multitude of art objects manufactured by rote, produced by stencils or molds, swiftly throws discredit onto the very class of objects involved. People no longer take the trouble to distinguish original stylistic work from servile routine work. General disfavor soon consigns the best creations to oblivion, and the most enlightened artist, himself led astray by this feeling, will fear being charged with barrenness of invention if he reproduces in his works compositions of which all eyes are weary.

Nevertheless, it would be a vain hope to try to find forms preferable to those handed down to us by the people of antiquity both in the arts of the spirit and those of decoration and industry. It is not the case that their superiority in every genre is always to be attributed to power of imagination or of talent. It seems to us that in a great number of areas we see the power of reason dominant among them, and—more than is usually realized—reason is the guiding spirit of architecture, decoration and furniture design. Reason is also what takes the place of nature in these arts. To follow nature in that multitude of objects known by the term furnishings is to be able to follow the inspirations of pleasure while remaining under the command of necessity, never to let the necessary be sacrificed to the pleasant, in fact to make the necessary become pleasant while keeping inconspicuous its claim to become so. For the artist, the nature—that is, the true model—of every object, of every piece of furniture, of every utensil, is that rationality, utility and suitability that its purpose demands. Among all the characteristics of a chair, for example, some are dictated by the form of our body, by relationships of necessity or suitability that are so evident that instinct alone would guide us to them. That is what nature is in this area. What remains for art to do?—to refine the forms dictated by the requirements, to combine them with the simplest contours and to elicit from these givens of nature the decorative motifs that will adapt to the essential form without ever disguising its character or denaturing the principle that gave rise to those motifs. And yet, how often have we seen the ornament applied to a chair arm or leg usurping the place of that arm or leg, or scrollwork replacing the part to which it should have been accessory and, against all probability, supporting what should have been supported by solid parts?

A mere glance at those thousands of kinds of clocks, products without any real producer, and similar to those parasitic plants that are as abundant as they are useless, will convince you of the laughable results of the spirit of fashion—that is, the spirit that consults neither nature nor reason.

That spirit is the natural enemy of all those arts that have no tangible or visible model for imitation and whose true regulator is reason. That spirit infiltrates them with the weapons of skepticism and paradox, and when it has succeeded in making all the principles on which architecture reposes seem arbitrary, when it has once established pleasure as the sole aim to which everything should relate, the ideas of order and rule disappear; then the anarchy of caprice directs all the productions of the arts that are subordinate to the art of building.

Therefore, if it is important for those arts—for architecture—to preserve its principles, its rules and its purity, it is no less important for architecture to uphold the maxims of a taste founded on reason when forming, designing and composing all the objects with which it shares the concern for beautifying society and increasing its pleasures. We believe that, in view of this interrelationship of architecture and furnishings, the architect should not only avoid abandoning the direction of the latter to craftsmen's routine, but also, for the sake of art and his own honor, should take the greatest pains with an area of art whose good or bad use affects the very fate of the architecture.

Furnishings are too closely linked to interior decoration for the architect to remain indifferent to them. The spirit of decoration, divorced from that of construction and operating out of concert with the latter, will not stick at any sort of absurdity or nonsense; not only will it pervert the essential forms of the building, it will make them disappear. Mirrors indiscreetly placed, tapestry clumsily hung, will produce hollow areas where there should be solid areas, and solid areas where there should be hollow areas. Construction is to buildings what the bone structure is to the human body. It should be embellished but not completely masked. It is the construction that, in accordance with the region, the climate and the type of building, provides the motive for the ornament. Construction and decoration are intimately related, and if that relationship ceases to be evident, there is a flaw in the whole. The execution of the work, whatever its extent or size, will have no effect on the mind if the embellishment has not been provided for in the construction, if the primary form seems not to correspond with the accessories, if, in short, two different wills out of touch with each other have directed the completion of the work.

To the extent that we have succeeded in proving that nothing in the realm of art is inconsequential, that good taste and the principles of beauty should appear as clearly in the smallest productions of the imitative arts as in the largest, and that their strength and joint success depend on their mutual accord—to that extent we are justified in believing that we will be forgiven for attempting to maintain the taste that served as our guide by offering to the public the details of furnishings that make up this collection.

We repeat, our intention in publishing this work is not so much to show the fruits of our labors as to contribute by our example to the battle against the spirit of fashion, which disdains what exists because it has existed, and the spirit of innovation, which admires only what has not yet existed.

It is not a blind admiration that leads us to praise the taste and style of antiquity, to which we have tried to make our compositions conform. If all the ages and all enlightened people agree in awarding the palm to the people of antiquity in things pertinent to imagination and the feeling for truth, and if we loudly profess that they are our masters in that regard, at the same time we recognize that among us science has often compensated for the faults of art. In the matter of execution, in many ways, the modern industrial arts have acquired, and will continue to acquire, superiority over those of antiquity. Everything that depends on experience can only improve with time, and especially by applying the achievements of the physical sciences to the arts.

To support our contention, it will suffice to mention the metalwork, mirrors and glass used in our interior decorations.

France, and especially its capital, possess infinite resources of substances suitable for beautifying dwellings, and merchants bring in wood, stone and all the materials that industry and taste can desire. The numerous glass, metal and porcelain workshops within Paris or in its suburbs employ many skilled workers, but their talent needs to be controlled by good taste.

If the study of antiquity were to fall into neglect, soon all industrial productions would lose that regulating force which alone can give the best direction to their ornamentation—which in a way prescribes for each material the limits within which its claims to please should be restricted, which shows the artist the best use of forms and confines the variety of forms within a circle that they should never transgress.

For example, the material of which porcelain vases are made has such intrinsic beauty and value that this should compel the artist not to hide it, as is generally done, beneath falsifying glazes which, far from increasing its value, lessen it for people of taste. What is the good of the gilding with which all these vases are covered? Do they want people to think the vases are of gold? The trickery is clumsy, for gilded porcelain will never be as fine and precious as gold. It loses its own merits without gaining those of metal in the eyes of the beholder.

How much absurdity good taste—or, better said, good sense—can discover in the new artistic ways of decorating faience and porcelain! All those miniature scenes, all those landscapes, all those perspective views painted onto our plates are merely an incorrect use of the art of decoration.

The same can be said about those chairs whose seats and backs are historical paintings. All these misconstructions are only products of fashion, whose only rule is to recognize no rule, whose only rationale is a refusal to submit to reason.

Persuaded as we are that this sickness, which is that of modern taste and infects the productions of every art, must find its treatment and cure in the examples and models of antiquity—followed not blindly but with the discernment suitable to modern manners, customs and materials—we have striven to imitate the antique in its spirit, principles and maxims, which are timeless. We have never had the whim of producing Greek pieces in order to be "in the Greek style." We have believed it necessary in decoration to make a distinction between the objects to be ornamented and the reasons for the ornament, and, convinced that these reasons are universal and eternal, we have merely aspired to the honor of strengthening their authority.

The various works included in this collection will doubtless offer numerous subjects for censure. The exposition of our principles and motives that we have just made will perhaps serve us as an excuse. If it is found that we have made a number of sacrifices to the very taste we condemn, we sincerely hope that the reader will appreciate the difficulties in satisfying taste and reason at the same time in arts that are subject to so many special constraints.

As we have already said, our purpose in publishing this collection is not to offer our works as models to be followed, but simply to show the results of our efforts in an art to which we have devoted all our powers and which we have long practiced. We present these works as materials to be consulted, either so that their faults can be avoided, or so that readers can make as much use of them as seems proper for the purpose they have in mind. We hope that the number and variety of the objects will not be their sole merit, and that, after curiosity is satisfied, art may also derive some benefits from them.

Par Percier et Fontaine.

PLATE 1: Perspective view of the painting studio of *citoyen* J. in Paris.

GUERCINO · PAULO VERONESE · TITIANO · ANIBAL CARACIO · MICHEL ANGELO · RAPHAEL D'URBINO · LEON.DE VINCI · DOMEN. ZAMPIERI · PIETRO PERUGINO · AND. DEL SARTO · CINABUE

ATHENES · CORINTHE · DELPHES · SAMOS · SICYONE

SCULPTURE · PEINTURE

Par Percier et Fontaine.

*Face latérale de l'Atélier de Peinture du C. I.****

|——————| 8 Pieds.

|——————| 1 Mètre.

PLATE 2: Side wall in the painting studio of *citoyen* J. [At the top, names of painters; at the
left, names of Greek cities.]

Par Percier et Fontaine.

*Plafond de l'Atelier de Peinture du C.I.****

8 Pieds.

1 Mètre.

PLATE 3: Ceiling of the painting studio of *citoyen* J.

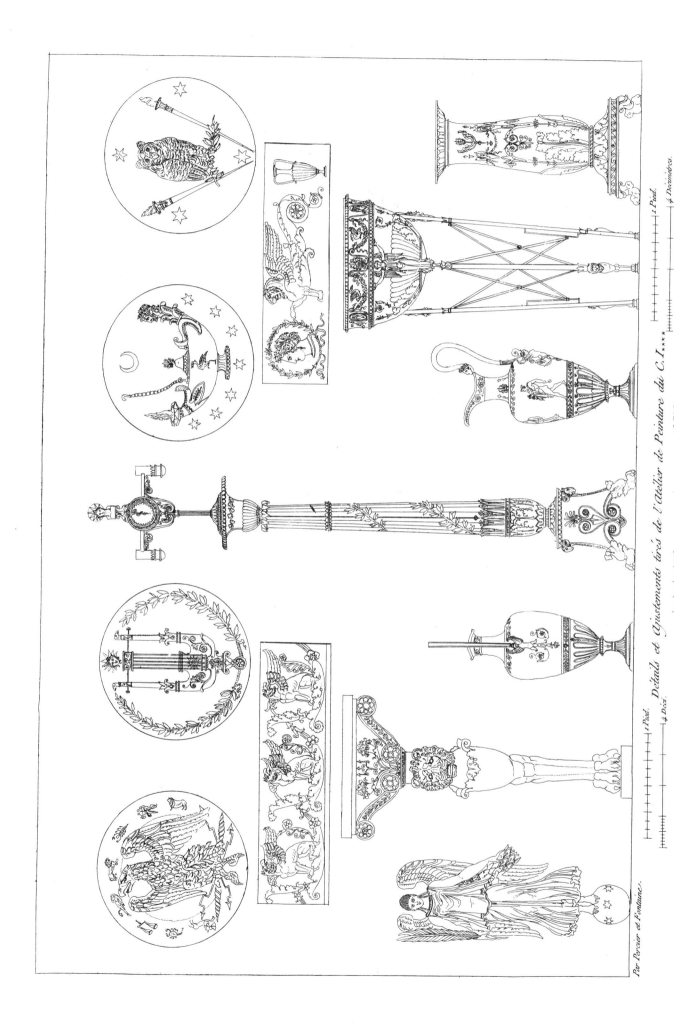

PLATE 4: Details and fittings from the painting studio of *citoyen* J.

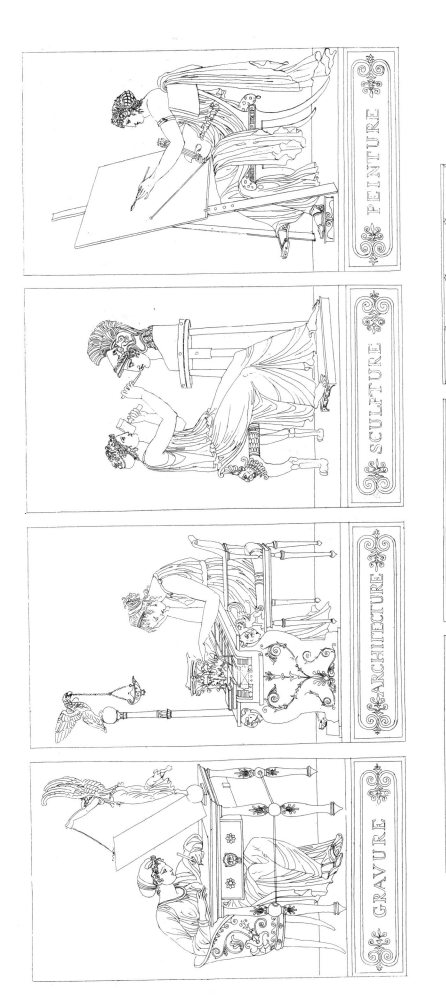

PEINTURE

SCULPTURE

ARCHITECTURE

GRAVURE

Par Percier et Fontaine.

*Panneaux et Frises de l'Atelier de Peinture du C. I****.*

— 2 *Pieds*

— 6 *Décimètres*

PLATE 5: Panels and friezes from the painting studio of *citoyen* J. ["Gravure" = Engraving.]

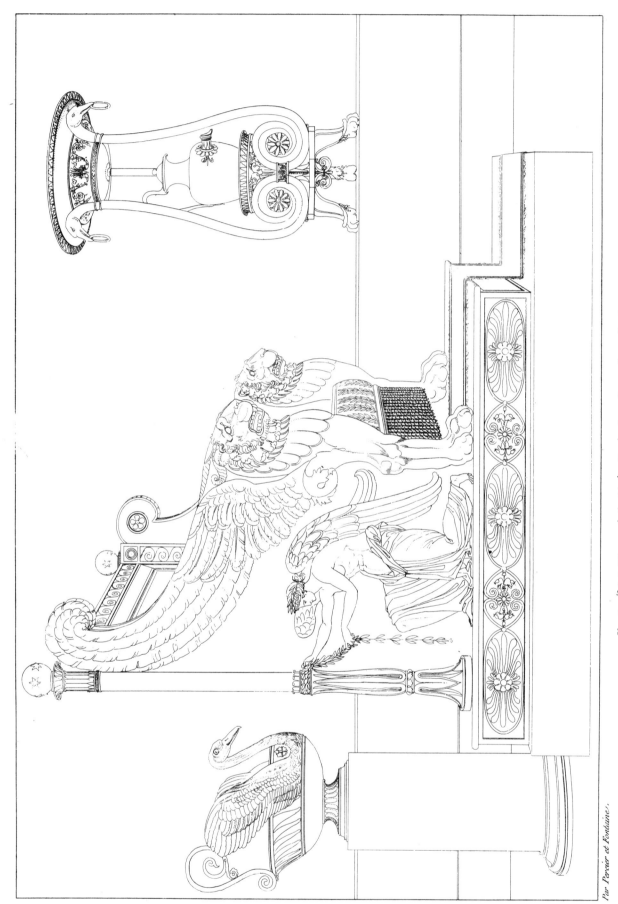

Fauteuil et Vases exécutés à Paris dans la Maison du C. D★★★★

Par Perier et Fontaine.

3 Pieds

1 Mètre.

PLATE 6: Armchair and vases for the home of *citoyen* D. in Paris.

Face latérale d'un petit Salon exécuté à Paris chez le C.C.

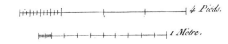

4 Pieds.

1 Mètre.

PLATE 7: Side wall of a small salon made for *citoyen* C. in Paris.

Par Percier et Fontaine.

Pendule exécutée pour le C. G. en Espagne ?

3 Pieds.

1 Mètre.

PLATE 8: Clock made for *citoyen* G. in Spain.

Cheminée exécutée à Paris pour le C.D.....

12 Pieds.

5 Décimètres.

PLATE 9: Fireplace made for *citoyen* D. in Paris.

Percier et Fontaine.

Jardinière ou Table à Fleurs exécutée pour le C.W. en Suede.

2 Pieds.

1 Mètre.

PLATE 10: Flower stand made for *citoyen* W. in Sweden.

Plan et Coupe de la Table indiqueé à la Planche précédente.

2 Pieds.

1 Mètre.

PLATE 11: Plan and section of the flower stand illustrated on the preceding plate.

Lustre exécuté dans la Maison du C. Ch......à Paris.

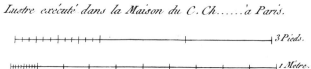

3 Pieds.

1 Mètre.

PLATE 12: Chandelier made for the home of *citoyen* Ch. in Paris.

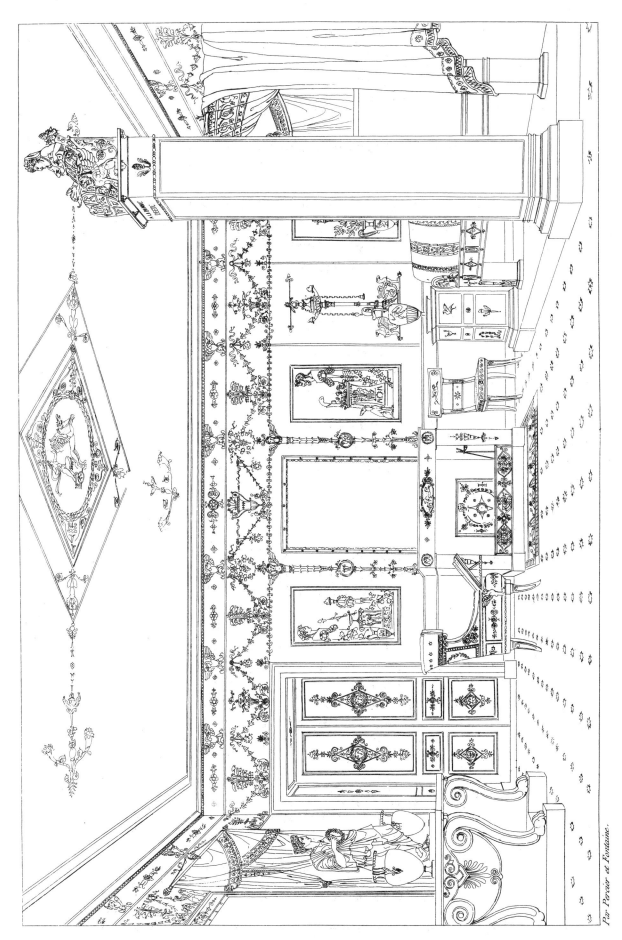

PLATE 13: Perspective view of the bedroom of *citoyen* V. in Paris.

Par Percier et Fontaine.

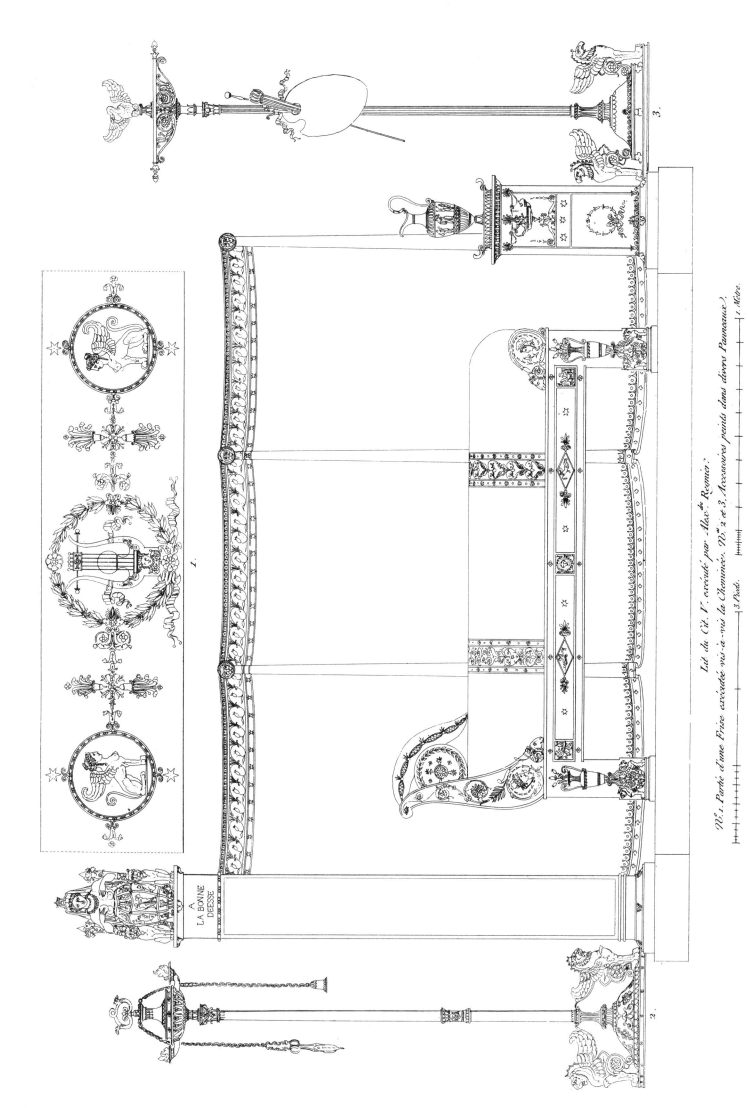

Lit du Cit. V. exécuté par Alex.dre Regnier.

N°.1. Partie d'une Frise exécutée vis-à-vis la Cheminée. N°. 2 et 3, Accessoires peints dans divers Panneaux.

├┼┼┼┼┼┤───────┤ 3 Pieds. ├┼┼┼┼┤────────┤ 1 Mètre.

Par Percier et Fontaine.

PLATE 14. *Citoyen V's bed,* made by Alexandre Regnier. (1) Part of a frieze opposite the fireplace. (2, 3) Panel paintings of items of furniture. ['A la Bonne . . . " = To the Good Goddess (the ancient Roman Bona Dea).]

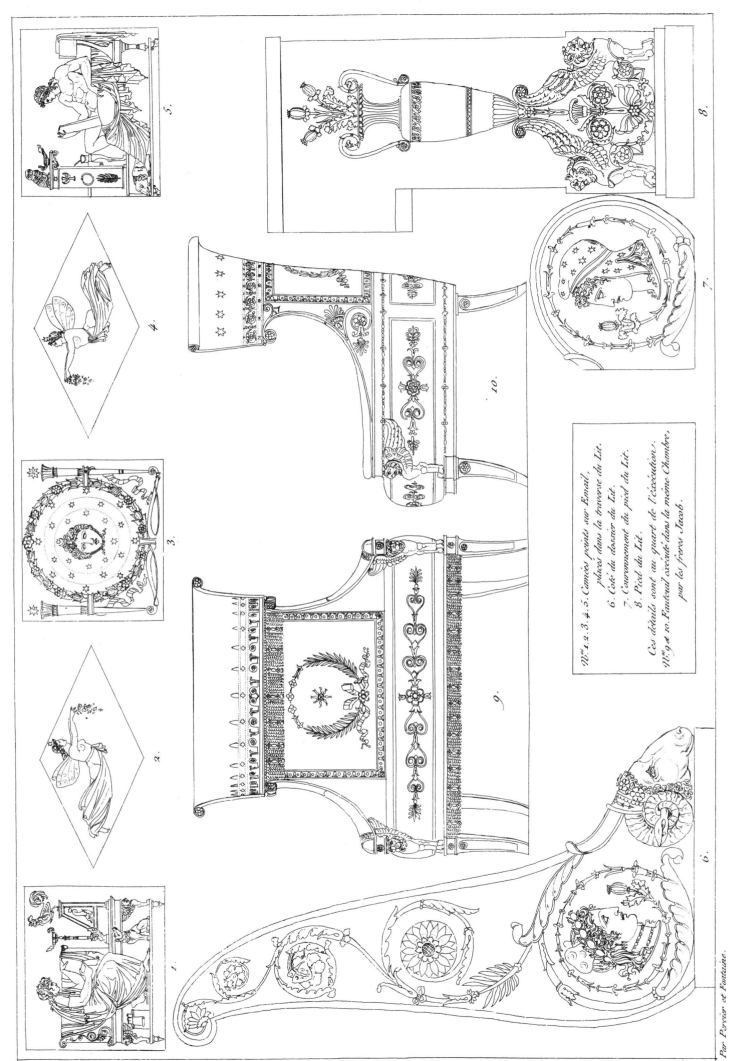

PLATE 15: (1–5) Cameos painted on enamel, set into the bed rail. (6) Side of the headboard. (7) Capping of the foot of the bed. (8) Foot of the bed. (6–8 are ¼ actual size.) (9, 10) Armchair for the same room, made by the brothers Jacob.

Par Percier et Fontaine.

N.os 1. 2. 3. 4. 5. Camées peints sur Email,
placés dans la traverse du Lit.
6. Côté du dossier du Lit.
7. Couronnement du pied du Lit.
8. Pied du Lit.
Ces détails sont au quart de l'exécution.
N.os 9 et 10. Fauteuil exécuté dans la même Chambre,
par les frères Jacob.

Par Percier et Fontaine.

PLATE 16: (1, 2) Panel paintings in *citoyen* V.'s bedroom. (3) Frieze in the same room. (4) Vase, ⅓ actual size. (5, 6) Front and profile views of a table made by the brothers Jacob.

1.

2.

3.

4.

Par Percier et Fontaine.

PLATE 17: (1–4) Panel paintings in *citoyen* V's bedroom.

PLATE 18: (1, 3) Dinner vessels for the home of *maître* ——— in Paris. (2, 4–11) Vases, lamps and incense burners for *citoyen* ——— in Paris.

Par Percier et Fontaine.

PLATE 19: Bed made for Mme. M. in Paris.

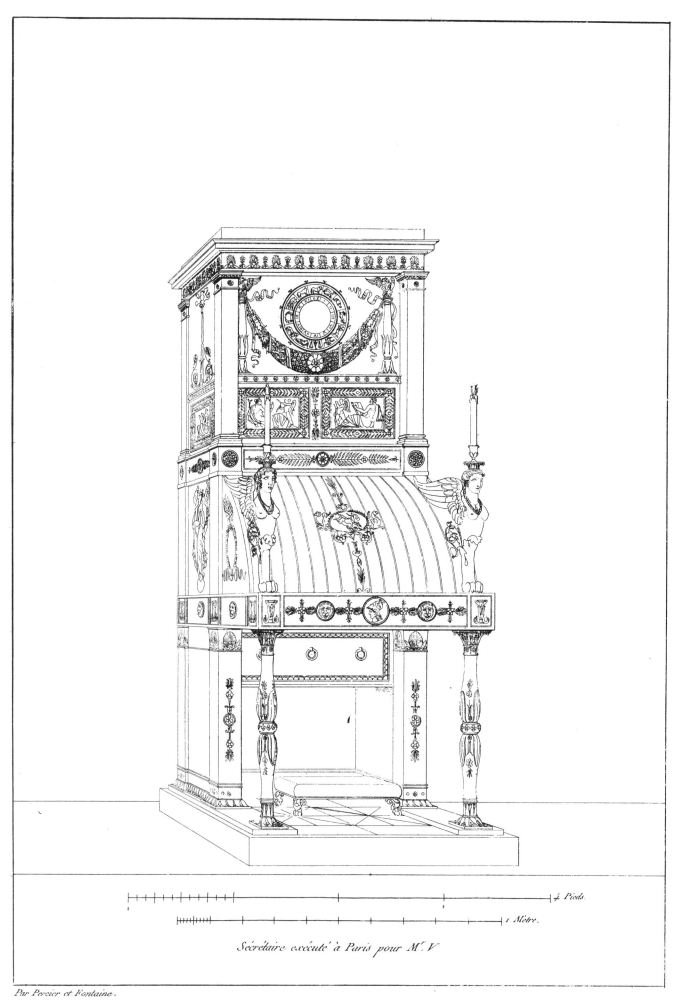

Secrétaire exécuté à Paris pour M.ʳ V

4 Pieds.

1 Mètre.

PLATE 20: Secretary made for Monsieur V. in Paris.

Dessus de la Table.

Par Percier et Fontaine.

2 *Pieds.*

1 *Metre.*

PLATE 21: Table made for Count S. in St. Petersburg. ["Dessus" = top of the table.]

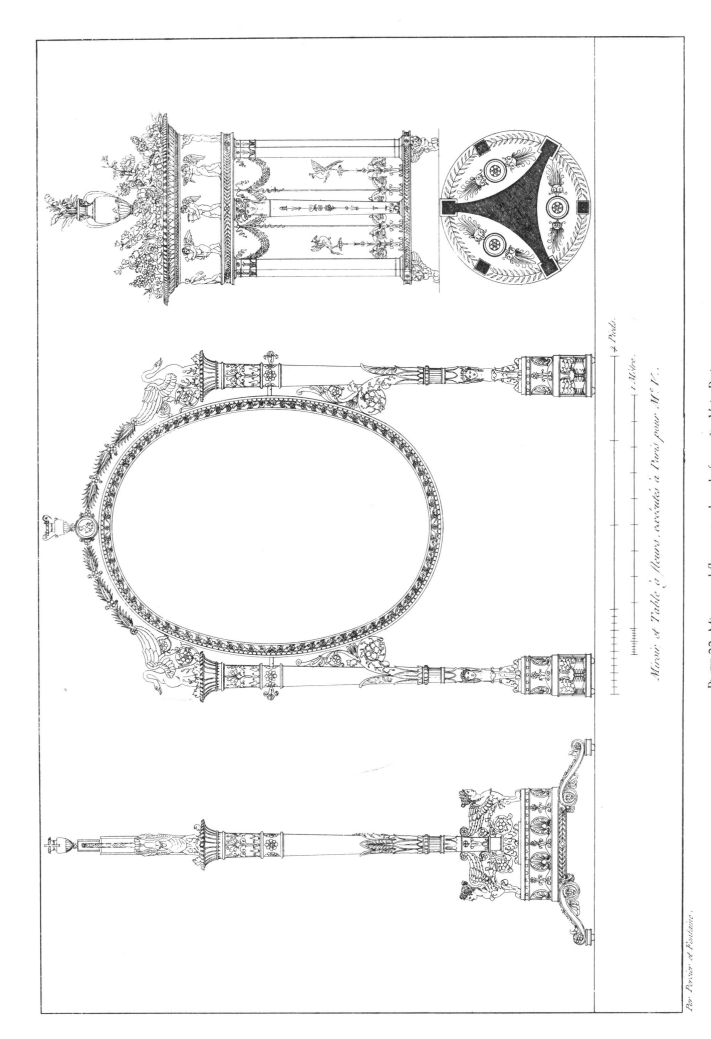

Miroir et Table à fleurs, exécutés à Paris pour M.ᵉ V..

4 *Pieds.*

1 *Mètre.*

PLATE 22: Mirror and flower stand made for *maître* V. in Paris.

1 Pied.

4 Décimètres.

Petite Table de travail,
renfermant une Cassolette,
exécutée pour M.ᴹ.à Paris.

1 Pied.

5 Décimètres.

Table de nuit,
exécutée à Paris pour M.ᴹ.
par les freres Jacob.

2 Pieds.

1 Mètre.

Candélabre exécuté chez M.ᴰ.à Paris.

PLATE 23: (LEFT) Small worktable containing an incense burner, made for *maître* D. in Paris.
(CENTER) Candelabrum for the home of Monsieur D. in Paris. (RIGHT) Night
table made for *maître* M. in Paris by the brothers Jacob.

PLATE 24: Table made for Count S. in St. Petersburg.

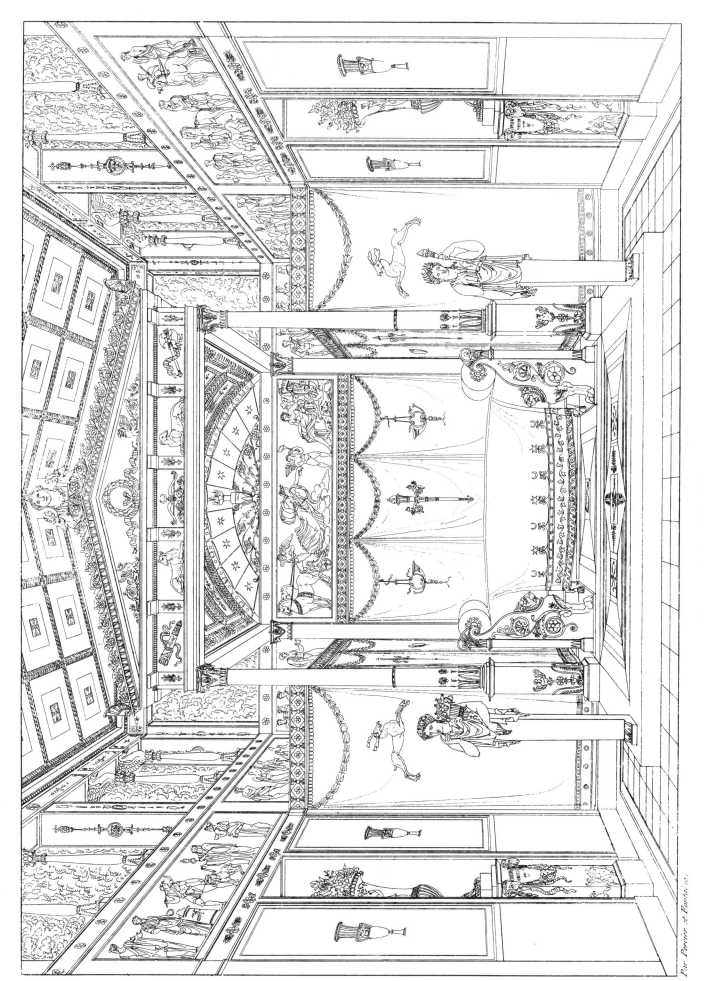

PLATE 25. Bed made for Monsieur O. in Paris.

Par Percier et Fontaine.

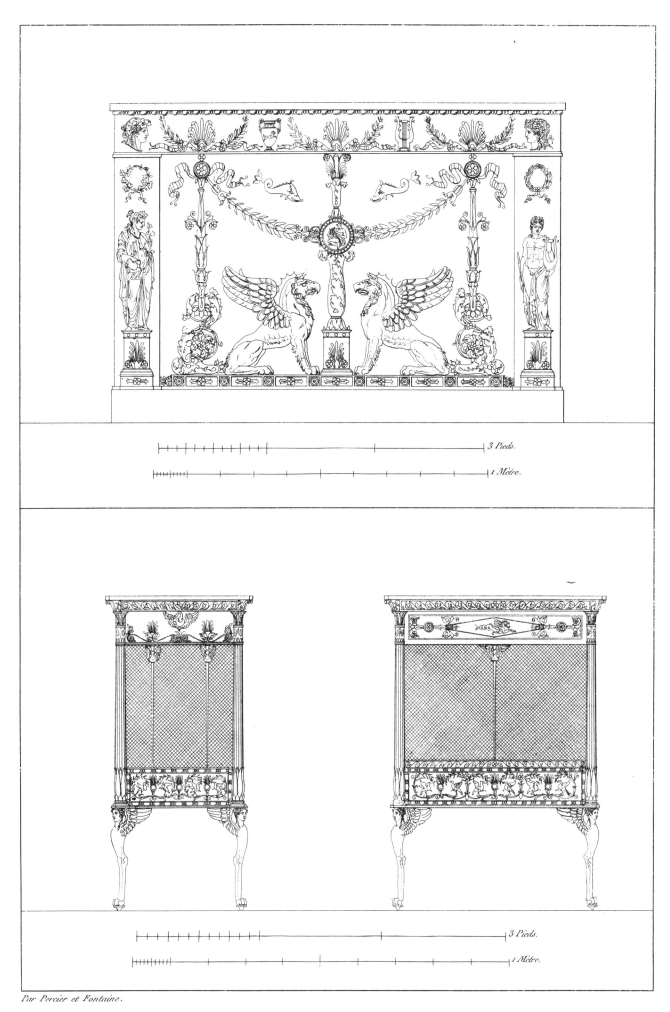

Par Percier et Fontaine.

PLATE 26: Commode and worktable made for Mme. de M. in Paris.

Cheminée exécutée chez M.r D. à Paris.

Avec le détail en grand du Basrelief au milieu de la traverse du Chambranle.

Par Percier et Fontaine.

PLATE 27: Fireplace made for the home of Monsieur D. in Paris, with a larger detail of the bas-relief in the center of the mantelpiece.

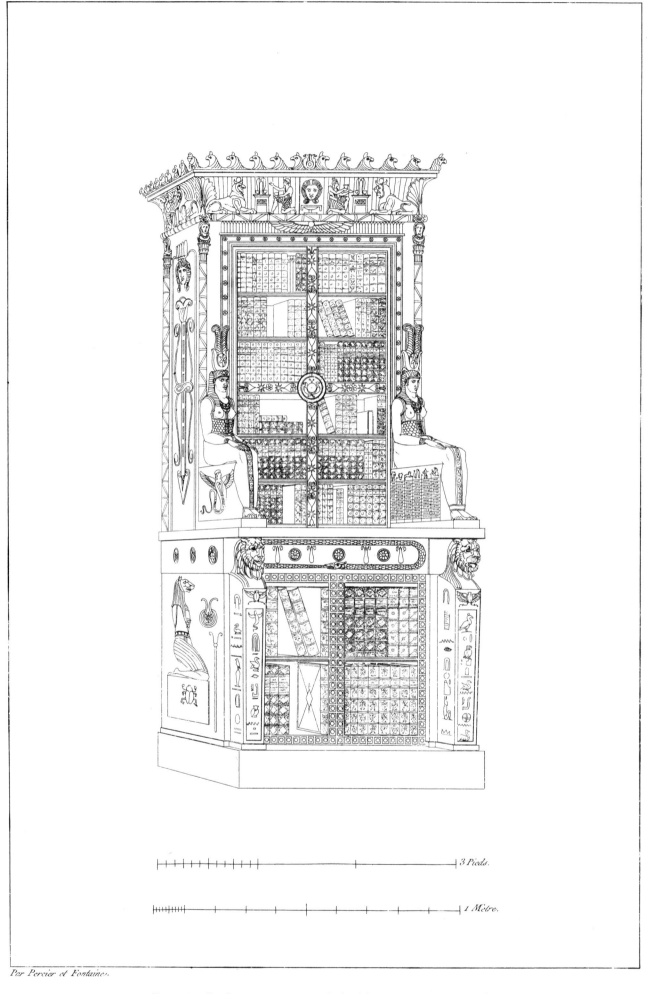

PLATE 28: Bookcase/secretary made for Monsieur V. in Amsterdam.

Fauteuil et Siege à deux places,

éxécutés à Paris, pour M. le C.^t de S. en Russie.

PLATE 29: Armchair and loveseat made in Paris for the Count of S. in Russia.

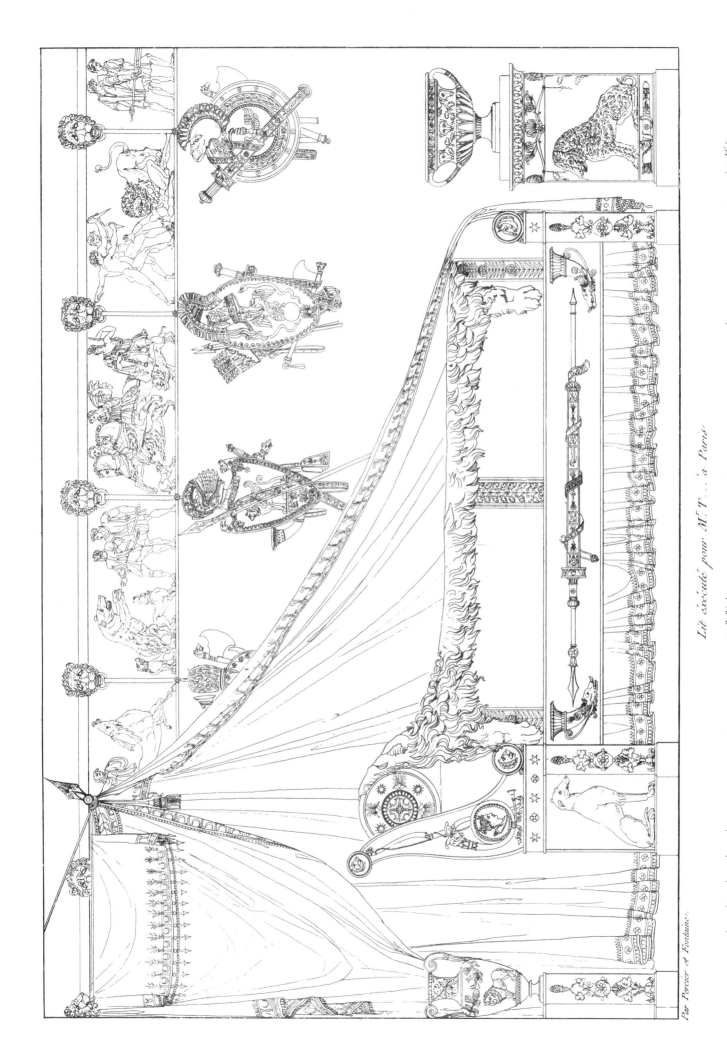

Lit exécuté pour Mr T... à Paris.

Par Percier et Fontaine.

3 Pieds.   1 Mètre.

PLATE 30: Bed made for Monsieur T. in Paris.

Par Percier et Fontaine.

PLATE 31: Fireplace with mirror backing in the gallery of Prince S. in Poland.

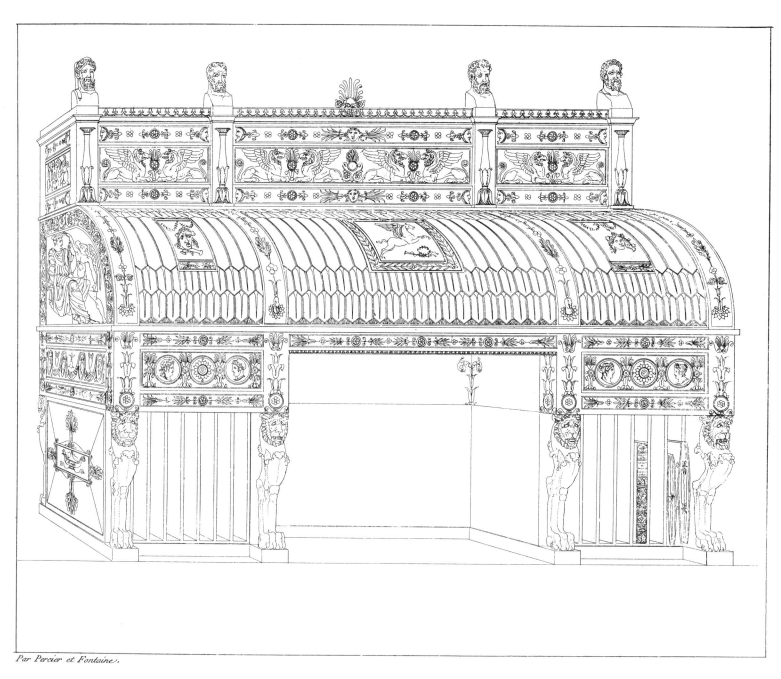

Par Percier et Fontaine.

PLATE 32: Rolltop desk made for Monsieur H. in Paris.

PLATE 33: Tripod, vases and frieze made for the home of Monsieur M. in Paris.

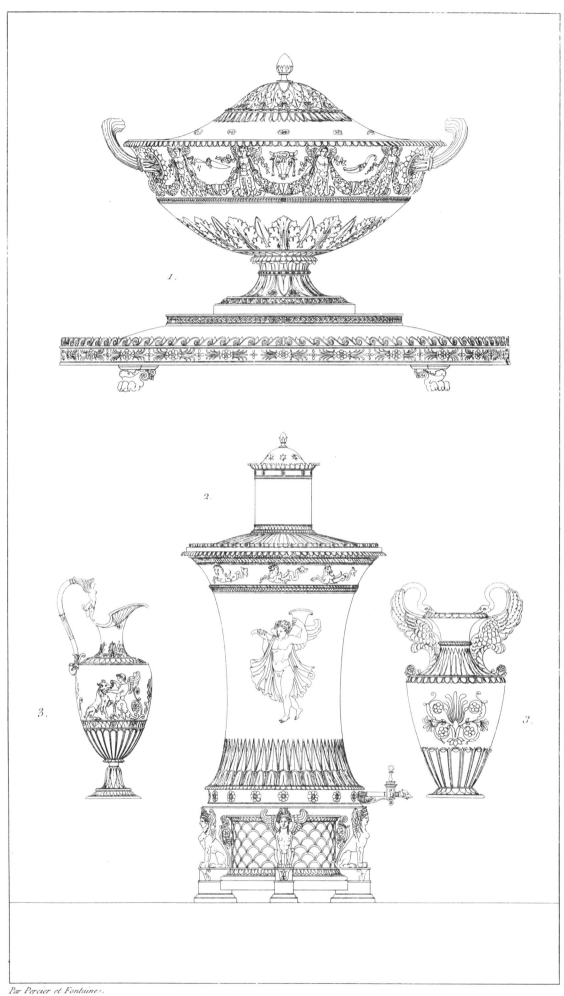

PLATE 34: (1) *Oille* vessel for a dinner service. (2) Tea urn. (3) Vases made for *maître* B. in Paris.

Par Percier et Fontaine.

PLATE 35: Porcelain table top made at the National Factory at Sèvres for *maître* B.

Par Percier et Fontaines.

PLATE 36: Bedroom made for Monsieur G. in Paris.

PLATE 37: One wall of Mme. G.'s bedroom in Paris.

Ch. Percier et Fontaine.

Ch. Percier et Fontaine.

PLATE 38: (1) Desk made for Monsieur V. in Paris. (2) Bronze vase made for Monsieur V. (3) Side view of the desk, No. 1. (4) Clock intended to support a bust.

PLATE 39: (1) Bergère-type armchair made for Monsieur de D. in Paris. (2) Armchair made for Monsieur L. in Paris. (3) X-stool made in Paris and installed at St.-C [loud]. (4) Candelabrum made for Mme. B. in Paris. (5) Side view of the X-stool, No. 3. (6) Small clock made for Monsieur W. (7) Table made for Mme. B. in Paris. (8) Table made for Mme. de G. in Paris.

PLATE 40: (1) Commode with drop front, made for Mme. de M. in Paris. (2) Table made for
the Count of P. (3) Commode with drawers, made for Monsieur du R. in Paris.

PLATE 41: Ceiling of the library at Malmaison.

Ch. Percier et Fontaine.

PLATE 42: Perspective view of the library at Malmaison.

Dévelopement de la Voute de la Salle à Manger du Palais des Tuileries.

PLATE 43: (ABOVE) Two-dimensional view of the ceiling vault of the dining room in the Tuileries palace. (BELOW) Transverse cross section of the dining room in the Tuileries palace.

Jardiniere exécutée à Paris pour M.E.★★

Par Percier et Fontaines.

PLATE 44: (ABOVE) Flower stand made for Monsieur E. in Paris. (BELOW) Tea table made for
Monsieur G. in Paris.

Par Percier et Fontaine.

PLATE 45: Ceiling of the guardroom in the Tuileries palace.

Détail en grand, de l'une des Anses du Vase ci-dessous.

Par Percier et Fontaine.

PLATE 46: (ABOVE) Larger detail of one of the handles of the vessel below. (BELOW) *Oille*
vessel made in Paris for H. M. the Empress [Joséphine].

PLATE 47: Ceiling of the throne room in the St.-Cloud palace.

PLATE 48: View of the Emperor's throne in the Tuileries palace.

Par Percier et Fontaine.

PLATE 49: View of the tribune and part of the Hall of Marshals in the Tuileries palace.

Lit exécuté pour M.^r Oz.....à Paris.

Par. Percier et Fontaine.

PLATE 50: (ABOVE) Bed made for Monsieur Oz. in Paris. (BELOW) Panel decorations in
Monsieur Oz.'s quarters.

PLATE 51: Ceiling of the small service salon in the Empress' rooms in the Tuileries palace.

Lampe.

Métier à broder.

Sceau à laver.

Cassolete à parfums.

Boîte de Toilette.

Frise de la Chambre à coucher de Malmaison.

Par Percier et Fontaine.

PLATE 52: (ACROSS, THEN DOWN) Lamp. Embroidery frame. Washbasin. Incense burner.
Cosmetics box. Frieze of the bedroom at Malmaison.

PLATE 53: Ceiling of the Emperor's bedroom in the Tuileries palace.

Par Percier et Fontaine.

PLATE 54: Flower stand made for Monsieur Ex. in Paris.

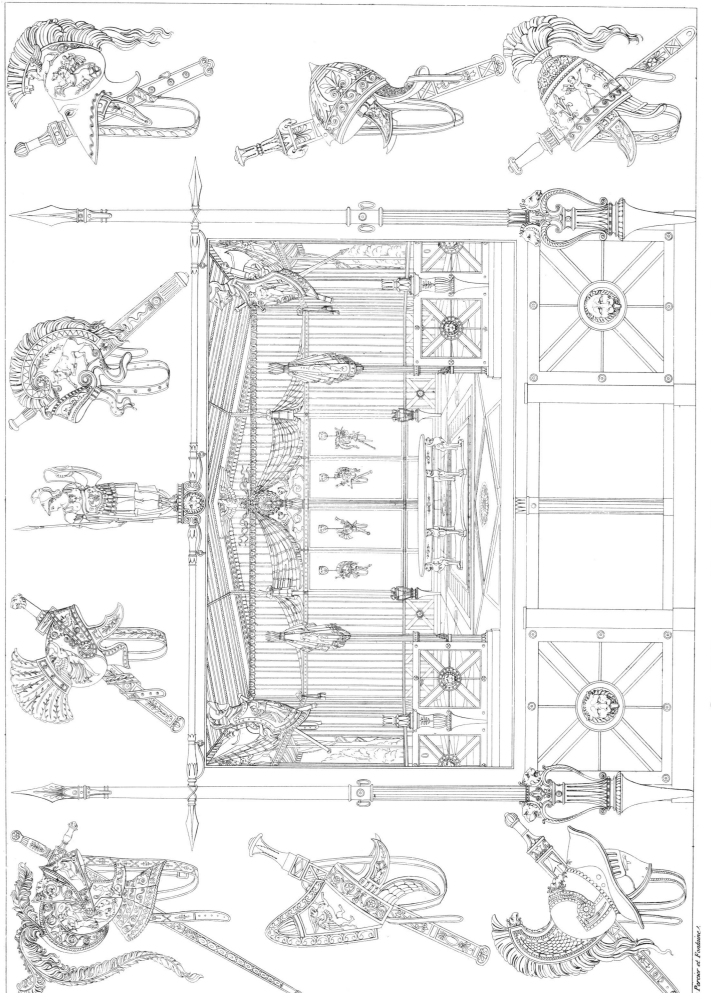

PLATE 55: Room in the château of Malmaison and details of its ornamental trophies.

Par Percier et Fontaine.

PLATE 56: Two-dimensional view of the ceiling vault of the foyer of the theater in the Tuileries palace.

PLATE 57: Fireplace made for the salon of Monsieur H. in Paris.

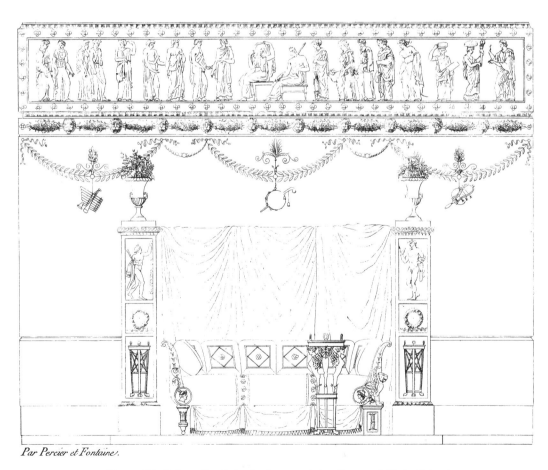

Par Percier et Fontaine.

PLATE 58: Side walls of the bedroom of the Count of Z. in Poland.

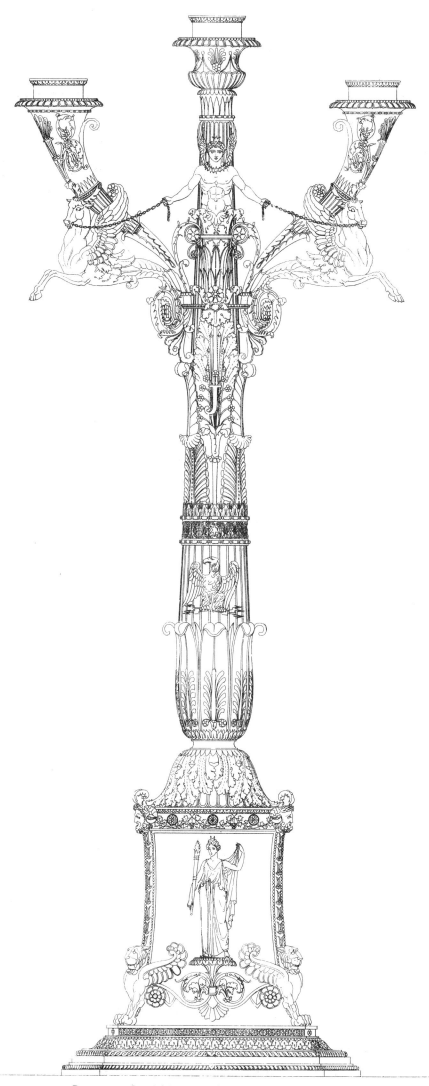

PLATE 59: Candelabrum with girandoles, made in Paris.

Par Percier et Fontaine.

PLATE 60: Boudoir of Mme. M., made in Paris.

PLATE 61: Interior view of a cabinet for the king of Spain, made in Paris and installed at Aranjuez.

PLATE 62: Entablature, capital and details from the cabinet of the king of Spain.

PLATE 63: Wall casing, armchair, tripod, vases and other accessories made for the cabinet of the king of Spain.

Par Percier et Fontaine.

PLATE 64: Two-dimensional view of the ceiling vault of the cabinet of the king of Spain.

Par Percier et Fontaine.

PLATE 65: Bed made for Mme. de B. in Paris.

PLATE 66: Fireplace of the grand cabinet of the Emperor in the Tuileries palace.

Par Percier et Fontaine!

PLATE 67: Perspective view of the Venus Room of the Napoleon Museum in the Louvre.

PLATE 68: Wall elevations of the Venus Room of the Napoleon Museum in the Louvre.

PLATE 69: Decoration of the ceiling vaults of the Venus Room of the Napoleon Museum in the Louvre.

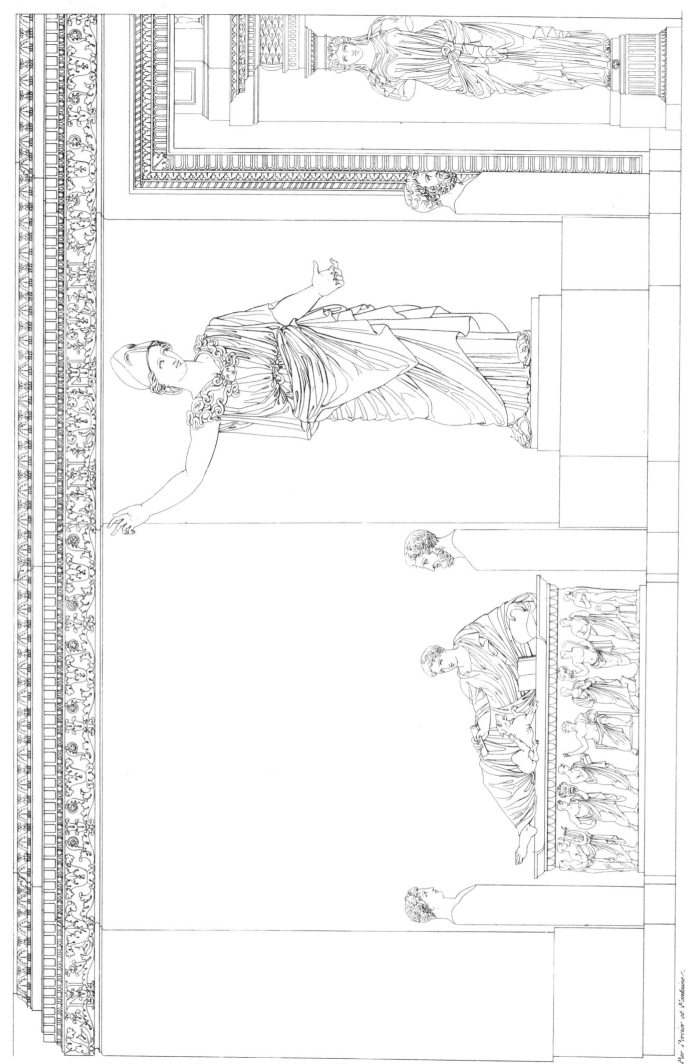

PLATE 70: Side wall of the Venus Room of the Napoleon Museum in the Louvre.

Par Percier et Fontaine.

PLATE 71: Ceiling vault decoration of the Venus Room of the Napoleon Museum in the Louvre.

Par Percier et Fontaine.

PLATE 72: Fireplace of the Rivers Room of the Napoleon Museum.

Explanatory Table of the Subjects Comprising This Collection

❦

PLATES 1–5
Interior view, section, ceiling and details of the decoration in the painting studio of Monsieur J. in Paris.

This room, the back of which is occupied by a bed raised on a dais, serves as both a workroom and a bedroom. Joinery pilasters separate the panels, on which are represented, in the Etruscan [ancient Greek] manner and on a brown ground, Painting, Sculpture, Architecture and Engraving. Above is a bas-relief frieze composed of figures of Fame and torches [flambeaux] supporting garlands; between the torches are medallions bearing the portraits of the most celebrated painters, with their names, countries of origin and birth and death dates. The stove, placed inside a terra-cotta pedestal covered with marble and bronze, supports a bust of Minerva. In front of each pilaster, a chimera foot forms a separate console for placing vases and utensils. On the ceiling, Apollo, symbol of day, is seen on the window side and Diana, symbol of night, on the bed side. The ornaments accompanying the principal subjects and comprising the details of this room are associated with the arts of design. They refer to the tastes and talents of the skillful artist for whom they were created.

PLATE 6
Large armchair for a writing desk, and vase for ablutions.

It can be seen from the shape of this armchair that it was made to stand in front of a desk. It is raised on a dais that is covered with fur on the part where the feet rest. Of the two furnishings that accompany the armchair, one was made of polished and gilded iron, the other of varnished sheet metal. The vase is of porcelain, the trim is of gilded copper.

PLATE 7
Side wall of a small salon executed in Paris.

The limited space and the situation of this room, which had to be made into a boudoir, led us to choose arabesque forms for its décor. It represents a little temple of Venus composed of light columns and decorated with various ornaments relating to the goddess of beauty. The entrances, which we tried to make inconspicuous, are hidden beneath draped hangings.

PLATE 8
Clock in Egyptian style, made for Spain.

The satiety produced by the great number of pieces of this class, and the desire to have an object that did not resemble all the rest, led to the request that this one be in the Egyptian style without attempting to denature the form necessary for the mechanism of ordinary clocks. We therefore confined ourselves to adorning the surfaces and outlines with signs and motifs drawn from Egyptian art. A head of Apollo, representing light, and two flanking sphinxes form the capping. The signs of the zodiac, indicating the months, encircle the dial. Two figures seated at the sides of the piece hold the keys to the Nile and represent time. Nature, in the form of Osiris, is depicted in the square, below which the movement of the pendulum is visible.

PLATE 9
Fireplace made in Paris.

This piece, built of veined white marble, is adorned with little figures that represent chariot races and with ornamented ormolu scrolls. We attempted to disguise the joins between the uprights and the cross piece by the projection of the fillet separating them. The cast-iron plaque behind the hearth is formed of several compartments; on the center one, we depicted Vulcan's forges. A gilded-copper openwork grille serves as a fender and replaces the usual andiron frontage.

PLATES 10 & 11
Flower stand for Sweden.

This table intended to carry flowers was made of mahogany, gilded copper, sheet metal and lead. Below the flower tray is a glass vase containing live fish, and above it is a cage or small aviary topped with a statue of Hebe. The bas-reliefs decorating the perimeter of the basket depict tritons sporting with naiads.

Plate 11 shows the plan and section of this piece.

PLATE 12
Chandelier made in Paris.

The owner already possessed the very few pieces of rock crystal with which this object was to be trimmed. He wanted to use them and requested that the richness of that material be matched by that of the bronzes and mounting. For that reason we thought of winged women holding hands in a circle and supporting torches encircled by garlands of brilliants of various forms. The women are raised on a foliage scroll from which spring winged griffins bearing candles on their heads. The mounting of this piece is carefully thought out and very simple; each part is constructed separately and is attached to the entire assembly by screws that are hidden by ornaments.

PLATES 13–17
View and details of a bedroom executed in Paris.

The ornaments decorating this room are painted in oil on plaster. Without any fixed theme, they fill various compartments of different sizes and shapes. Among them are still lifes of fruit and details of everyday objects, grouped together and painted in grisaille on light grounds. The furniture, the table facing the bed, the tripod, the washstand, the bed and the mantelpiece, details of which are shown on plates 14–17, are clad with bronzes, paintings on enamel and inlays of various kinds of wood. The pedestal, isolated at the head of the bed, is a closet for keeping nighttime clothing and objects.

PLATE 18
Dinner vessels.

These vessels were made of silver and silver-gilt for dinner services. We tried to make their shapes usable and, above all, easy to manufacture.

PLATE 19
Bed made in Paris.

Convenience of use was the chief goal we set ourselves when designing this work. This is why we called for shapes without any angle: everything in the outline of the head, rail and foot is rounded. The ornaments and the enamel cameos are set into the thickness of the wood. A wreath of flowers, mingled with poppies, carved, gilded and topped with white plumes, is suspended over the bed, forming its tester.

PLATE 20
Secretary made in Paris.

This small piece of furniture, intended for keeping books, documents and money, has a clock in its upper part; secret drawers below; and, in the middle, a rolltop and pullout slides for writing. Chimeras on either side of the table carry girandoles for candles. The piece is made of different kinds of wood and clad with bronze plating.

PLATE 21
Tea table.

The design for this table has been sent to Russia for construction in porcelain and bronze. The compartments and the ornaments that decorate the table top are to be painted in multicolor with grounds and highlights in gold. The principal subject is the birth of Amphitrite, who is surrounded by tritons and dolphins.

PLATE 22
Movable mirror and small flower stand made for the apartment shown in Plate 13.

The supports and entire framework of the movable mirror are of sections of ormolu covering an iron core. The feet rest on casters and the mirror is held by two pivots that allow it to be inclined at any angle. The small flower stand is designed for placement in the middle of a boudoir. It is a basket of varnished sheet metal ornamented with bronzes. It is supported by arabesque gaines (terminals) and by pilasters to which garlands are attached.

PLATE 23
Candelabrum, night table and small worktable.

The first-mentioned of these three pieces is of gilded wood; it was made to support a girandole. The second is made of mahogany and bronze.

On its principal face we depicted a dog, symbol of fidelity, and poppy-leaf ornaments, symbol of sleep. The little worktable is composed of a slide-out writing surface, a pan for burning incense and a gold-wire reticule hanging from the corners for storing needlework and other useful objects.

PLATE 24
Tea table designed for Russia.

It is raised on a plinth that serves as a base for a row of balusters, above which is a flat surface (miniature table top) with a porcelain vase in the center. Four terminals with gaines and eight arabesque bronze columns, resting on chimera heads, support the table top and the incense burner.

PLATE 25
View of a bed and a part of the room in which it is situated.

The smallness of the room that we were to decorate and its shape—much greater in length than in width—led us to conceive of decorating the bed as a small temple of Diana. Its lightweight top is supported by four small arabesque columns raised on pedestals. The ceiling compartments and the divisions of the cornice and the frieze are decorated with emblems and attributes relating to Diana. A bas-relief at the back of the bed shows this goddess being guided by Love to the arms of Endymion. The terminals in front of the dais represent silence and night. Two cloth hangings, to the right and left of the first column, cloak the entrance to the privies made possible by the isolation of the bed. The ceiling of the room, which slopes to follow the angles of the top of the bed, seems to be supported by pillars with spaces between that permit a view of the leafy trees in the midst of which this imaginary small temple was erected.

PLATE 26
Commode and small table made in Paris.

The front of this commode, the panels of which are of mahogany decorated with ormolu ornaments, opens to its full width by means of iron pivots placed in the thickness of the wood. The sliding drawers remain hidden behind and are thus better protected from air and dust. The table, two views of which are given, is composed of four small bronze columns, the bases of which rest on chimeras. The panels of the four sides are openwork gilded brass grilles, and the exterior of the drawer above is decorated with gilded copper inlays.

PLATE 27
Mantelpiece with its ornaments.

Almost all fireplace cladding is composed of several pieces of marble attached by iron or copper clamps, which, held together by gums or cements, often come apart from the heat of the fire. The uneven joins produced by this effect are quite unpleasant to see. Therefore we simplified the design of this mantelpiece and concealed the joins of the uprights beneath the copper medallion and in the corner of the cross piece. We were also careful to put cladding over the copper edging near the hearth to avoid the breaking to which it is subjected.

PLATE 28
Secretary serving as a small bookcase.

The Egyptian form we adopted had been requested in order to display a varied group of rare woods and to provide motifs for different inlays. The two seated figures and the two terminals with Osiris heads are of bronze.

PLATE 29
Armchair and loveseat made in Paris.

In the design of these two pieces we attempted to combine richness, comfort and charm. Almost throughout, the wood is rounded and covered with embroidered fabric, silk, wool and gold.

PLATE 30
Bed made in Paris.

Its shape and arrangement and the design of the accessories sufficiently indicate that it was made for a military man who is a great hunter. Weapons of different types and wild animal skins are used as decoration. A bow and arrow attached to the ceiling hold up the draped material that keeps out the air and insects at night. The painted bas-reliefs behind the bed depict animal hunts.

PLATE 31
Fireplace in front of a mirror.

The architecture of the gallery at the end of which this fireplace is installed consists of an Ionic colonnade of marble columns and pilasters. The mirror, which occupies one of the intercolumniations and in front of which the fireplace remains an isolated furnishing, infinitely repeats the décor of the room and multiplies its lavish ornamentation.

PLATE 32
Fireplace in front of a mirror.

This piece, like the majority of those in the preceding plates, was made in the workshop of the brothers Jacob in Paris. It is of mahogany, trimmed with bronze and a variety of marquetry. The interior contains pigeonholes, secret drawers and several very useful partitions.

PLATE 33
Tripod and vases.

The tripod, the shape of which may recall one of those found in the excavations at Herculaneum, serves as an incense burner in private living quarters. It is raised on a small marble pedestal decorated with bas-reliefs depicting chariot races.

PLATE 34
Oille dinner vessel, tea urn and vases made of silver and silver-gilt.

These metal utensils were made with extreme care and refinement. The separately cast and engraved ornaments are attached with great skill to the areas for which they were designed. It is impossible to praise too highly the ability of French craftsmen in this type of work.

PLATE 35
Porcelain table top.

The Sèvres factory, wishing to give an example of its most perfect manufacturing methods, planned the execution of a very large table top in one piece. To decorate the upper surface it was decided to paint the love of Helen and Paris in the center, with various secondary subjects related to the main one.

PLATE 36
View of a bedroom.

The decoration of this room, one of the least lavish in this collection, consists of the design of its fireplace, formed of coupled pilasters supporting an arch. Two sets of bookshelves fill the space between the pairs of pilasters on either side of the fireplace. The rest of the room is hung with gathered draperies over which valuable paintings are displayed. The large motif painted within a circle of stars above the hangings behind the bed represents Diana on a chariot; her wings spread, she covers the earth with her veil.

PLATE 37
Side wall of a bedroom.

From the richness and abundance of ornament in this decorative scheme it is clear that it was designed for a lady's bedroom. The preceding plate shows her husband's room. Comparing them, it will be seen that one, hung with wool drapery, has for decoration only paintings, and books placed between pilasters on either side of a fireplace. The other room has a sequence of pilasters, between which very decorative tapestries are suspended from the architrave of the order. An elaborate frieze, composed of scrollwork, chimeric figures and garlands, runs around the top of every wall. These decorations, which have some relation to the attributes of the Graces and Beauty, are multicolor paintings on light grounds, heightened with gold.

PLATE 38
Desk, clock and vase.

This desk, consisting of two stacks of drawers and standing on four bronze chimera feet, is made of mahogany with inlays of various materials. The actual clock, although it is the raison d'être of the piece in which it is installed, is only a secondary feature. It appears on one side of a pedestal intended to support a vase or a statuette. The bas-relief above the dial depicts Apollo; the one below it shows the Hours encircling Time in their round dance. The small vase, made of silver, was intended as part of a dinner service and is used as a salt cellar.

PLATE 39
Candelabrum of gilded copper for holding four air-current [Argand] lamps. Tea table standing on a bronze column and on thin scrolls of foliage. Table standing on winged-chimera feet. Small clock with a dial borne on an eagle's wings, the seasons being depicted in bas-relief on the pedestal. Large armchair and bergère covered with embroidered velvet panels. Folding X-stool.

It should be noted that on these different everyday furnishings we attempted a thorough subordination of the decoration to the conditions demanded by utility.

PLATE 40
Two very elaborate commodes.

The first one is covered with panels that open and that conceal the drawers. The decoration is of bronze and mother-of-pearl. The second has visible drawers; its ornaments are also of bronze. The round table, number 2, intended to be placed in the center of a salon, is an imitation of those ancient tables the fragments of which were preserved in the Vatican Museum.

PLATES 41 AND 42
View and details of the ceiling of the library of the First Consul at Malmaison.

The nature of the location that had been chosen for this library necessitated its division into three parts and was the reason for the arrangement of Doric columns forming open spaces and supporting arches that form a sort of lunette or spandrel. In the middle of the two circle segments that terminate the rows of columns, at the east and west, there is on one side a French door leading to the main path of the garden, and on the other a fireplace with a clear sheet of glass affording a view of the countryside. The main ceiling motif represents Apollo and Minerva. The portrait heads depict the most famous authors of antiquity, and the names of those whose works serve as models [of literature], wreathed in laurels, fill the other parts of the vaults.

PLATE 43
Decoration of the ceiling vaults and of one of the (spandrel-like) arched openings of the dining room in the Tuileries palace.

To some extent, the depressed shape of these vaults and of the lunettes that intersect them determined this scheme of subdivision into arabesque compartments. A sequence of coupled pilasters bearing arches forms the decoration of the room. Mirrors placed between each two divisions infinitely repeat the lavishness of the ceiling and the movement of the whole ensemble. This arrangement, which adds greatly to the splendor of the space, is also intended to give more light to the room which, although fifty feet long, could only be illuminated by a single casement.

PLATE 44
Tea table and flower stand intended to be isolated at the center of a room.

These two pieces were made of mahogany and bronze. Their high degree of finish and the perfection of their workmanship are clear indications that they are from the workshop of the brothers Jacob.

PLATE 45
Ceiling of the guardroom in the Tuileries palace.

This ceiling, the square part of which is supported by upright covings, is painted in grisaille with gold highlights and imitations of bronze on varied grounds. The main motif represents Mars, weapons in hand, traversing the globe on his chariot and marking each month of the year with a memorable victory. Trophies, in the center of which imperial eagles can be seen, decorate the center of each of the four planes. Seated Victories present palm branches or inscribe the name of the victor, and warlike Virtues support the garlands that frame the main motifs.

PLATE 46
Metalwork oille *vessel for the dinner service of Empress Joséphine.*

It received special notice at one of the public exhibitions of products of French industry, as much for the perfection of the engraving as for the skill with which its component parts were assembled.

PLATE 47
Ceiling of the throne room in the château of St.-Cloud.

The compartments, decorations and scenes of this ceiling are painted in grisaille with gold highlights on grounds of different colors. The bas-reliefs at the center of each coving represent the Emperor's weapons, to which all ranks and ages of society do homage. The center of the square part of the ceiling is decorated with a large painting representing Truth, by Monsieur Prud'hon.

PLATE 48
The Emperor's throne in the Tuileries palace.

It is the golden seat covered with dark violet velvet, adorned, as is the hassock, with bees and ornaments embroidered in gold. It is raised on a dais of three steps, with a carpet of crimson velvet embroidered in gold. A carved and gilded wreath of laurel and fruit, surmounted by a helmet and with a very lavish trimming of white plumes, forms the top of the canopy. The drapery or imperial mantle, of crimson velvet sprinkled with bees and with embroidered fringes and borders, is lined with violet satin. In the center above the throne are seen the arms of the Emperor, embroidered in gold and raised in relief. The mantle hangs from the wreath and joins up with two imperial standards, composed of wreaths, ornaments and eagles in the round, and placed on gold bases on either side of the throne. It is around these standards and at the foot of the dais that the civil and military officers who comprise the Emperor's court gather and stand during the ceremonies.

PLATE 49
Views of the tribune in the Hall of Marshals in the Tuileries palace.

This room, one of the largest in the capital, was long used as a guardroom. Today it is reserved for festivities and grand assemblies. It is the main salon in the palace. The portraits of the marshals of the Empire and the busts of generals who died serving the State decorate the interior. The tribune that adorns the wall on the garden side is formed of four caryatids, copied from the one made by Jean Goujon for the guardroom of Henri II in the Louvre. It conceals the assemblage of two large stoves that heat this vast space. The balcony of the tribune is reached by two small circular staircases, which are contained within the thickness of the walls and which also lead to the gallery that circles the room at the level of the balcony.

PLATE 50
Bed and details of ornaments.

A garland of poppies is attached to two candelabra that conceal the two corners at the head and foot. Two recumbent sleeping female figures are depicted on the front panels. The bedspread and the two bolsters that receive it are lavishly embroidered in gold on a velvet base.

PLATE 51
Part of the covings of one of the ceilings in the Empress' rooms in the Tuileries palace.

This ceiling is painted in grisaille with gold highlights on gray, violet and blue grounds. It is divided into compartments adorned with scrollwork, horns of plenty and garlands. Muses and Cupids are the principal motifs of the framed elements, and in the center, on the square part, an old painting of Apollo and Ceres was placed.

PLATE 52

The small pieces of everyday furniture shown on this plate have been reproduced several times, even with some variations, by Parisian manufacturers. They may be regarded as commercial furniture. The embroidery frame, the cosmetics box, the washbasin and the lamp have been executed to the same designs, but in materials of varying costliness. We do not think it necessary to explain their construction in detail. This aspect of their design, with regard to the present plate and all the similar ones that precede it, would require too extensive a description. We have limited ourselves in each case to a brief statement of just what is necessary to identify their use and artistic composition.

PLATE 53
Ceiling of the Emperor's bedroom in the Tuileries palace.

The coat of arms and monogram of the Emperor, with military trophies and garlands supported by figures of winged genii, comprise the surrounding decoration of this ceiling. Four Virtues, in the symbolic form of the four principal deities of ancient mythology, are painted in grisaille with gold highlights on lapis-lazuli grounds. They occupy the centers of the four bands on the square part of the ceiling.

PLATE 54
Flower stand to be placed in the center of a large room.

It is an elaborate planter supported by terminal figures that surround an aviary, around which are tiny fountain basins. Children in a round dance are depicted on the basket that springs from the center of the planter. The entire ensemble is crowned by a statuette of Flora that seems to emerge from the flowers.

PLATE 55
View and details of a salon created for the château of Malmaison.

The First Consul had requested a council chamber. The installation and decoration had to be completed in ten working days because of the desire not to interrupt the frequent journeys there that he was accustomed to make. Therefore it seemed appropriate to adopt the form of a tent supported by pikes, fasces and standards, among which are suspended groups of weapons that recall those of the world's most famous bellicose nations.

PLATE 56
Part of the ceiling vault of the foyer of the theater in the Tuileries palace.

This ceiling, the subdivisions of which are enriched with coats of arms, scrollwork, garlands and fruits, is painted in grisaille with gold highlights on a gray, violet and blue ground. Within the frames of the large compartments are depicted the four major rivers of France and, on the perimeter, the medals of the principal cities of the Empire.

PLATE 57

In the particular form of the ornaments that compose the ensemble of this fireplace we tried to avoid acute angles, which are often very inconvenient in daily use. The Victories and weapons that decorate the piece have reference to the profession and qualifications of the person for whom it was made.

PLATE 58

The decoration of this bedroom is only part of the decoration of a vast château that was being restored. The designs were sent to Poland. The proprietor, a man famous for his knowledge and an outstanding connoisseur of works of antiquity, wanted his bedroom to be more noteworthy for the simplicity of its arrangement than for the lavishness of its ornament. The bed is an imitation of ancient beds. A bas-relief frieze encircling the room is reminiscent of Greek ceremonies and customs.

PLATE 59
Large candelabrum, made of gilded copper, meant to be placed in a corner of a salon and to hold girandoles of lights with several branches.

PLATE 60

This plate represents a wall opening in a boudoir opposite a casement, with a davenport, built into the back of which are two small pigeonholes, for placing books, and a clock in the center. In the background, through a clear glass, are seen the greenery of a garden and a white marble statue.

PLATES 61–64

This cabinet, of modest dimensions, was completely manufactured in Paris and shipped to the palace of Aranjuez in Spain. Every element of it is made with extreme care and precision. Mirrors cover the lunette compartments, increase the extent of the vault and infinitely repeat the rich wall decoration. The panels are of mahogany and the ornaments of platinum [actually, silver- and gold-plated bronze]. The large paintings, depicting the Seasons, that fill the spaces between the pilasters, as well as the medallions showing children's games, are by Monsieur Girodet. The small paintings of the most beautiful geographic sites are by MM. Bidault and Thibault. The ensemble of this room, the furnishings and details of which are the subject of plates 62–64, presents an extraordinary richness.

PLATE 65
Bed with a wreath-shaped tester supported by two arabesque gaines that terminate in busts of small winged figures.

The draperies and fringes beneath which the curtains hang are attached to the wreath. The woodwork of the bed is adorned with winged children who support horns of plenty filled with fruits and poppies.

PLATE 66
Fireplace of the grand cabinet of the Emperor in the Tuileries palace.

The decoration of this fireplace was designed to match that of the room, which was executed during the regency of Anne of Austria [1643–1651]. The cornice moldings, and the ornaments of the wall casing and the existing ledge furnished the motifs for the new scheme. The marble bas-relief above the fireplace, in the center of which is a clock, represents History writing to the dictation of Victory. The arms and monogram of the Emperor are the subject of the other decorations.

PLATES 67–71
Perspective view, elevation of the principal wall, vault on the same side, lateral elevation and two-dimensional view of the ceiling vault of the room in the Louvre where the Venus of the Napoleon Museum is to be placed.

This room, one of the most lavishly decorated of those containing the masterpieces of ancient sculpture, has marble cladding. The vaults are carved and gilded; the motifs with which they are adorned are emblems and attributes of the fine arts, in different forms.

Plate 72
Fireplace of the Rivers Room of the Napoleon Museum.

The two statues that form the principal group in this arrangement once decorated the fireplace of the guardroom of the Louvre. They are from the hand of Jean Goujon, who sculptured the four beautiful caryatids supporting the tribune that stands at the opposite end of that room. Changes in construction required that these two beautiful pieces be moved. They were placed in storage. When the Louvre was restored and its lower rooms devoted to the exhibition of masterpieces of ancient sculpture, it was thought advisable to take advantage of the opportunity offered by the completion of this room and, to the extent that it was possible, to return things to their original state and, in the decoration of the fireplace as in all the other elements, to recall the artistic taste of the era of Henri II. That is why the motifs for the new ornaments were derived from the work of Jean Goujon and Pierre Lescot, deservedly famous artists who, in the reign of Henri II [1547–1559], were placed in charge of the constructions at the Louvre, and to whom we are indebted for the most remarkable features of this palace.